Insights from the Boardroom

Insights from the
Boardroom

Herman Daems on
Corporate Governance

Contents

What this book is about

WHAT DOES THE BOARD OF DIRECTORS OF A LIMITED LIABILITY company or not-for-profit organisation actually do? What does the board chairman or woman do? What exactly is expected of a board member? And how is the role of a board of directors or, to use a more academic term, a governing body, likely to change in the future? These are all questions which I address in this book. I have in fact been wrestling with some of these points for many years and, to be perfectly honest, I still haven't entirely made up my mind about everything. However, I am far enough along the road with my thinking to be able to put forward some useful answers.

Due to a chain of circumstances and coincidences, I have for a number of years had the opportunity to sit on the boards of some 25 European and US companies and organisations, serving as chairman of the board for eight of these. They come from an extremely wide variety of sectors, ranging from finance to technology, infrastructure, manufacturing and the world of publishing. They include not only established corporations but also startups and organisations in the health and cultural sectors. The experiences that I've had have made me think hard about my real role as a director or chairman of the governing bodies of the various companies and organisations in which I served.

A board member or chairperson must certainly do 'something' that creates added value. This sounds reasonable enough, but what exactly does it mean? What is the added value of a governing body or an individual director who sits on it? And for whom should this added value be created? In order to answer these questions, I started to think about the role of a governing body and how it can be made to work well.

Entire libraries have already been written about what these days is generally known as 'corporate governance'. Many of these books are prescriptive, i.e. they set out what a board ought to do. They say very little about what board members really do or can do. Moreover, most of the books and articles on this subject are written by lawyers or other authors who have themselves rarely had the experience of sitting on a board. The lawyers tend to set out with hair-splitting precision what the law requires of a board and the individual directors, their duties and responsibilities, but they don't say what happens in reality. A governing body not only has to deal with legal questions but also with practical issues for the running of the organisation. However, corporate governance experts usually concern themselves primarily with what directors are required to do, not with what they actually do or don't do.

Let's take an example. In order to drive a car on the road, you need a good knowledge of the Highway Code. You need to know what the various road signs mean, how fast you're allowed to drive, who has right of way in what situation, and the conditions a person needs to fulfil in order to be able to drive a vehicle. All this is very important. Without the Highway Code, safe driving would be practically impossible. However, the Highway Code tells you nothing about how to actually drive a car. A person who knows the Code by heart will not necessarily be able to start the car engine, let alone drive the vehicle and park it without causing any damage. These skills have nothing to do with simply knowing the contents of the Highway Code.

> A person who knows the Highway Code will not necessarily be able to drive a car. The situation in the boardroom is very similar.

It's clear, however, that the one is not possible without the other. And just as someone who has an excellent mastery of a car will not be able to drive it safely without a good understanding of the rules of the road, a person who has the appropriate skills for a board member will not perform well in terms of corporate governance unless s/he understands the duties and responsibilities of a director. You can't have one without the other.

This book is not about laws and codes. It's about what directors do or ought to do in practice. The book is based on what experience has taught me. But right away I have to disappoint anyone who's looking for revelations or exposés. My aim is not to write an account of my own experiences but to try to provide useful insights on the basis of those experiences.

I am, of course, fully aware that experiences represent only part of the truth and that laws and codes are also a vital element. In fact, I would be unlikely to have any other opinion on this, given that I'm a former chairman of the Belgian Commission on Corporate Governance which drew up the 2009 Belgian Corporate Governance Code. However, creating added value as a board member implies much more than simply obeying the law or following a code. It calls for insights into the real role and workings of a corporate governance body.

My insights are based on the experience that I've been gathering continuously from 1990 to the present day. This has been a significant period. When I first became a director at various enterprises and organisations in Belgium, the corporate governance movement was in full swing, resulting in the Belgian Corporate Governance Code for companies listed on the stock market and the highly influential Buysse Code – drawn up by Count Paul Buysse – pertaining to unlisted businesses. Governance codes have been fully applicable during the greater part of this period, but we were still working with the 'old' Belgian company law. Now there are new developments in the law and in the Belgian Corporate Governance Code, which are likely to lead to different experiences. Here I'm thinking mainly about the option for Belgian-based companies that wish to introduce a 'two-tier' governance system, i.e. with separate supervisory board and management board.

Nevertheless, I believe that the recent changes to the legislation and the Code make very little difference to the insights that I put forward in this book. There are two reasons why I believe this. First of all, as chairman of a large Belgian bank, I've had long experience of working with separate supervisory and management boards. Banks in Belgium have been required to work this way for decades. Moreover, as chair of the governing body of the University of Leuven, I'm perfectly accustomed to working with a two-tier board structure. I've also had the chance to experience the workings of a two-tier board system at Netherlands-based companies.

The second reason is of a different kind. Although Belgian companies now have the legal option of introducing a split board structure, I'm not yet convinced that the majority will actually choose to do so. In particular, when a business is in the hands of controlling shareholders who like to keep their fingers firmly on the pulse, there will be no great pressure to bring in a two-tier board. Nor do the professional managers in Belgium have the power or influence at this moment in time to impose a two-tier approach on their shareholders. It will however be interesting to see whether state-owned enterprises opt for a two-tier structure.

The new *Belgian Code of Companies and Associations* (BCCA)[1] provides that members of the board must direct all their actions towards achieving the purpose or object of the company or not-for-profit organisation. This is a clear duty, but the provision is so wide that it offers very little practical guidance. It's as if you were to tell a pilot that s/he must do everything to keep the aeroplane in the air. S/he clearly has a duty to do so, but this tells you nothing about what exactly the pilot can and must do in order to keep the plane

---

1   The term used in Belgian law – vereniging (NL) or association (FR) – confers a specific meaning on the word 'associations', relating to the fact that while these organisations may make profits, they are not owned by shareholders who have the right to appropriate the profits made and/or sell their rights to future profits in the form of stock or shares.

flying. I therefore intend to give more concrete form to the general duty *"to do everything necessary in order to achieve the object"*[2] of the company or organisation, by breaking it down into four core tasks: setting the course for the organisation; supervising/monitoring the management; setting standards and promulgating corporate values; and taking responsibility/being accountable for what happens at the firm or organisation.

There are factors other than legislation or the principles laid down in codes that determine why corporate governance bodies differ sharply in the way they carry out these four central tasks. For instance, regardless of what the legislation lays down, some boards are more geared to taking on a course-setting role, while others lean more towards the purely supervisory aspect. Why is this? Quite simply because the context in which boards work varies considerably. One important contextual factor is the shareholder structure. Later in the book, I'll explain the experiences I've had with different shareholder structures. It can make a very big difference whether you're a board member at an enterprise in which one family or a particular group has virtually total control or whether different branches of a single family or various other shareholders are involved. If the company is listed on the stock exchange, that of course also makes a difference, but the simple fact of being listed doesn't in itself explain everything. An additional question is whether or not a listed firm has controlling shareholders or a major shareholder among its stockholders. A further difference arises when the state holds a stake in the company. The shareholder structure is therefore certainly one factor that helps to determine the way the board works, but there are other factors as well. I'll be dealing with these in some detail in this book.

My main conclusion is that there isn't only one single type of governing body in existence. There are literally hundreds, differing widely from one another. This doesn't mean that every governing body is

---

2 The BCCA speaks of 'object' rather than 'purpose'.

carrying out an entirely different set of core tasks from all the others, but rather that there will be variations in the relative importance of the four core duties that I listed above. These variations help to determine the way in which each governing body works in practice.

So what are the foundations on which a governing body is built? What issues need to be settled and what agreements must be reached so that a governing body can work properly? The main factors here are, inter alia, the composition of the board of directors, the role and workings of the committees that advise the directors, the style of meetings, the allocation of tasks between the chair, the board members and the management, plus the way the chairperson and the chief executive officer (CEO) or general manager work together. In this book I'll be discussing these building blocks and showing how the context in which the company or organisation works is of crucial importance for the various components.

In the first three chapters, I'll describe the core tasks, the context and the building blocks of a governing body. In so doing, I'll try to show what a governing body actually is. In the following chapters, I'll attempt to clarify how a governing body works. I'll describe in turn the matters that a board discusses, decides and approves, what the chairman or woman does or can do, and how a board meeting is run.

A governing body or board is a meeting point where people representing various interests come together to make collective decisions about the course the company or organisation should take and the resources needed to do so, and also to assess whether the resources allocated are being properly used. Whenever different people and different interests confront each other, tension will always arise. Such friction is not necessarily a sign of failures in the organisation, though this cannot, of course, be ruled out. However, even in the most successful organisations, you can't avoid some blustery weather at the top. It's a simple fact that around the boardroom table you'll find a range of interests, opinions and characters. In my experience, friction surfaces when the various players at the top of the organisation don't stick to their appointed roles or don't perform those roles in a proper manner, for instance when the chair behaves like a CEO or board members act as if they were managers. Later on, I'll argue that you can avoid friction at the top of the organisation if everyone fulfils the role that s/he is supposed to play.

While most people usually know very little about what a board of directors does, they generally know even less about the role of the board chair. I therefore devote an entire chapter of the book to this subject, inter alia explaining the difference between a board chairperson and a chief executive. It must be clearly understood that the chief executive officer is the captain of the corporate ship. The task of the chair is then to ensure that the CEO is able to steer the ship properly and that the vessel stays on course in the event of a storm. In the United States, companies often prefer to have everything in the hands of one leader, appointing a single person to perform both these jobs with an impressive title such as Chairman & CEO. In Europe, these posts are usually allocated to two different people. I personally advocate this latter approach. I don't see any danger of dog-fights breaking out in the boardroom as long as the chair and the chief executive understand and accept the fact that each of them has a different role to play. It's perhaps not so different from the theatre; if one actor steals lines that belong to a fellow actor in the play, there's bound to be trouble!

One of the most difficult tasks of a board of directors is knowing what you need to know. There's a kind of paradox here. The directors are supposed to know everything in order to be able to fulfil their core duties but, quite obviously, they cannot know absolutely everything about what goes on in the organisation. The board has to wage a permanent struggle not to be left in the dark about what's happening. Governance is all about managing your ignorance. In this book I'll talk about the numerous tools that have been developed to keep the directors informed about the real issues facing the organisation. However, perhaps the most important factor here is trust between the directors and the management. If there's a

Governance is all about managing your ignorance.

high degree of trust, managers will spontaneously inform the directors about what's going well and what isn't.

So what exactly is expected of a board member and how can someone become a good director? The very least that can be expected of a board director is that s/he will form an independent opinion about the matters that the board has to deal with. Moreover, s/he must express that opinion: silence is not an option. At the same time, s/he should also understand that the discussions that take place in the boardroom on a given subject must lead to a decision. The company or organisation needs to move forward. Serving as a company director is something that appeals to a lot of people. Many think they fit the bill but not all of them grasp what the job is all about. As a director, you don't have the satisfaction of leading a group of people. You can't just roll your sleeves up and go to work. You make decisions, you give your approval, you assess, advise and encourage, but you don't get to taste the fulfilment that comes from hands-on implementation, because that side of things is the province of the CEO and the management. Being a supporter of a sports team is not at all the same thing as being a player.

In the final chapter, I speculate about how governing bodies are likely to evolve and how the directors' job is going to change. I foresee that both for-profit companies and not-for-profit organisations will in the near future undergo a transformation that will not leave their governing bodies unaffected. There are a number of reasons for these expected changes. First and foremost, our society is changing and there are calls for more transparency and greater engagement with society. Some companies and organisations will be expected to explain more clearly what they're doing and why they're doing it. There are now loud calls for corporations in the financial industry and the health sector, plus also digital technology and data companies and any business that has a high impact on the environment or the climate, to give a full account of their actions.

The disruptions brought about by digital technology are also bringing about quite a lot of governance-related changes within organisations. The need to have a clear 'purpose' – a key concept which I shall explain later in the book – is going to become of great importance for both for-profit companies and organisations without profit motive. Sometimes there will have to be a trade-off between purpose and profit, as several experts including Oxford economist Professor Colin Mayer, Larry Fink – the renowned CEO of Black Rock, one of the largest investment funds in the world – and Financial Times editor Andrew Edgecliffe-Johnson have argued in various books and opinion pieces. Readers will be aware that the famous dictum of the late Nobel Prize winner Milton Friedman that "the social responsibility of business is to increase its profits" has taken a hefty knock in recent years.[3]

Companies and organisations will increasingly have to deal with four basic issues: 1) how is control over the company organised? 2) who bears the risk arising from the decisions that are taken? 3) how is the supervision of a company or organisation that has raised funds from third parties organised? and 4) what is the purpose of the company or organisation? It has generally been standard practice to leave these four issues to the shareholders. Legal structures have been developed and introduced precisely for this purpose. Now we're seeing the start of a bifurcation. Especially in the United States, companies issuing non-voting shares are being set up. In such cases, some shareholders consequently have no say in the running of the business but they still bear part of the risks. We're also seeing company structures with similar effects being established in Europe. Once it becomes possible to confer multiple voting rights on some of the shareholders, that creates a dichotomy between having control and bearing risk,

---

3   Collin Mayer – *Prosperity. Better Business makes the Greater Good*. Oxford University Press, 2018; Larry Fink – *Purpose & Profit. Larry Fink's 2019 Letter to CEOS*, BlackRock; Andrew Edgecliffe-Johnson – *Beyond the Bottom Line: should business put purpose before profit?*, Financial Times, 4 January 2019; Milton Friedman – *The social responsibility of business is to increase its Profits*, New York Times Magazine, 13 September 1970.

which then poses special challenges for the board of directors. On the one hand, the board has to cope with the fact that, in such cases, control over the company is more streamlined, while on the other hand the board needs to take care that non-voting investors, who bear some of the risks, are protected against any irresponsible or reckless behaviour on the part of the management and the shareholders who exercise control over the company. This will inevitably lead to boards becoming more professional.

In the financial sector some people envisage a sort of certification system for directors. The proponents of this approach see it as a logical extension of the existing procedures intended to subject directors of financial institutions to what are known as 'fit and proper' assessments – i.e. continuous assessment of whether a bank board member is a suitable person, from both a knowledge and behavioural point of view, to carry out his/her directorial duties. Will we see further expansion of this kind of requirement for directors? I don't know, but I wouldn't rule it out, given that the wider society would certainly like to see more governing bodies being able to perform their central duties in a more expert and standardised manner. However, this approach may well have its drawbacks. If companies and organisations are to work successfully, they need to be able to draw on diverse skills and experience. Creating a caste of professional board directors is unlikely to be conducive to meeting this need.

Acknowledgements

A large number of business leaders, heads of organisations and company shareholders have directly or indirectly contributed to the opinions that I have set out in this book. I'm quite sure that not all of them will agree with what I've written in these pages. I offer my sincere apologies to those whose ideas I haven't followed and to any who are taken by surprise by some of my more daring pronouncements. I can however assure them all that their ideas have profoundly influenced my views. I hope that the new ideas I'm putting forward here, especially in the last chapter, will make this book an interesting read, not only as an intellectual exercise but also as a practical guide to running a company or organisation.

Since 1990, I've served as chairman or board member of some 25 companies and organisations in Europe and the United States and have consequently been involved in a good number of business sectors, including chemicals, glass, high tech, software, publishing, as well as banking and insurance, private equity and venture capital. Five of those companies were listed on the stock exchange or launched on the stock market while I was chairman or a director. Meanwhile, the not-for-profit organisations on whose boards I sat brought me into contact with healthcare, the cultural sector and higher education. The average period during which I served as a director at these organisations has been six and a half years, my 15-year tenure of the board chair at a listed technology corporation being the outlier here. In total, I have been – or still remain – chairman of the governing body of eight companies or not-for-profit organisations.

I'm also familiar with the workings of committees reporting to governing bodies: I've chaired audit committees, remuneration committees and hiring committees and served as a member of strategy committees and risk committees. All in all, I've had the opportunity to build up broad experience, in terms of both the number of companies and the number of different sectors in which I've served as a director.

The people whom I'd like to thank first are the chairs of businesses and organisations that gave me the opportunity to sit on their boards. Next, I'd like to thank those chief executives of Belgian and foreign companies and organisations who placed their trust in me, firstly as a director and later on as chairman. I sincerely hope that I've never betrayed their trust and that I've been able to give them some useful support. In addition, I owe acknowledgement and a large debt of thanks to the members of the governing bodies which I've chaired. I very much hope that our board meetings have borne their fruit in building up those enterprises. My sincere thanks also go to the shareholders of family businesses for whom I served not only as a board director or chairman but also as a reliable confidant.

I would also express my thanks to those loyal investors who used to attend the general meetings of shareholders. Being able to meet up every year at the AGM helps to engender mutual respect. A special word of thanks here to the senior management of the BNP Paribas Group and its Belgian arm, BNP Paribas Fortis. It has been a truly unique experience for me to serve as chairman at a major subsidiary of a global banking corporation.

Last but not least, my thanks go to KU Leuven, where I've had the opportunity to do practically everything – study, teach, publish and latterly also to chair the governing body.

I also gained considerable experience and picked up a lot of ideas during my chairmanship of the Belgian Corporate Governance Commission from end-2008 to 2013. A big thank-you to all the members of the Commission for what I learned from them.

I'd also like to express my appreciation to the hundreds of attendees at the seminars on corporate governance that I've given at IESE in

Barcelona and at the joint Harvard Business School/ IESE programme for company directors. The questions, remarks and real cases that so many international participants have brought up over the years have really helped me to formulate my opinions. Sincere thanks to all of them, and especially to the IESE management, who have always supported me and involved me in their international initiatives.

Meanwhile, my contributions at the international conferences in New York on Inclusive Capitalism and Long-Term Capital, and on the Future of the Corporation at the Montreal Forum helped me to reflect more deeply on the ongoing changes in society and the influence they're exerting on business enterprises.

Moreover, I have to acknowledge a considerable intellectual debt to the hundreds of board chairpersons and chief executives who took part between 2010 and 2017 in the annual Corporate Governance Summit run by the Deloitte professorial chair at KU Leuven.

If you want to publish a book, you need ideas. However, those ideas will turn into a readable book only when you've written a readable text. In this process, I've benefited enormously from the support of a small but dedicated editing committee, whose members have undertaken a critical reading of the text. I'll never forget the intense discussions we've had at the Ducale House in Brussels. Many thanks to this loyal and highly committed editing team. They have done their utmost to prevent me from making any errors, whether in my thinking or spelling and grammatical constructions. If any uncorrected inaccuracies remain in the text, these are entirely my own responsibility.

Sincere thanks also to my personal assistant at the Bank and the excellent team working at my publishers, LannooCampus. Without their dedication, patience, encouragement and professional support, this book would never have seen the light of day.

I have just one more person I'd like to thank: my wife Mariëlle. Without her patience and support, these *Insights from the Boardroom* would never have become available to you, the reader.

Herman Daems

CHAPTER 1

The core duties of a board of directors

Little-known and poorly understood

What the governing body of a for-profit company or an organisation without profit motive does is not generally well understood. Many people are simply unaware of the contribution these directorial bodies make to the workings of the economy and the wider society. However, they have a far-reaching remit and carry considerable responsibility. Below, I provide an outline of the core tasks of a board of directors.

THE BOARD OF DIRECTORS OF A BANK, A CHEMICALS PRODUCER, AN investment company, a technology enterprise, a hospital or a university is not closely involved in the day-to-day running of those firms and organisations. Boards and the directors who sit on them remain something of a mystery to the outside world. As I pointed out in the introduction, even friends and acquaintances of mine who work in the business world or inside an organisation sometimes wonder what the job of a company director consists of or what the tasks of a board of directors are. "So, what do these people actually do?" they will often ask.

However, even those working inside companies and organisations rarely know very much about their board of directors. The employees have little or no contact with them. Very often the staff don't even know the names of the individual directors, although there is certainly no secrecy about the composition of a board: the identity of the directors is publicly available information that can be found quickly and easily. Unfortunately, in this case as in so many others, ignorance tends to breed antipathy. Many people regard the board of directors as an out-of-touch and irrelevant body and some even view it as a threatening or hostile element, given that decisions taken by the board may be so far-reaching that they can have a negative impact on the career and indeed the entire future of any employee. Of course, in many situations, board decisions will have

> Out-of-touch, irrelevant and even hostile: this is how the board of directors is often type-cast.

positive outcomes, for instance when they promote expansion-oriented investment policies.

By contrast, the tasks of the chief executive officer and the management, who have hands-on responsibility for running the organisation, are much better understood. The CEO and the managers are usually better-known to the employees, have direct contact with them and feature more frequently in local or national news reports. Moreover, employees, customers and suppliers can more readily see and feel the outcome of decisions taken by the CEO and the management team. Most often it's the managers who set salaries and bonuses and conduct staff appraisals. The board will of course lay down the principles and policy guidelines for staff remuneration and appraisals but won't decide the salary packages of individual employees. However, the distinction goes much further than this. The impact of board decisions on the business and the organisation only really becomes clear in the longer term.

When company directors do feature in the news, it's usually because something has gone amiss, such as when a firm posts very poor results, embarks on a restructuring process, commits a serious transgression, breaks environmental rules or replaces its chief executive.

Sometimes criticism is laid at the door of the board regarding events in which the directors were not involved or of which they had no knowledge – instances of fraud or bribery, for instance. Moreover, if staff, without the knowledge of the management, sell products to particular customer segments for whom they are not appropriate – which may happen in the financial, medical and pharmaceutical world – the directors might not get to know about it immediately. Reports of such mis-selling or of other mistakes made by the company rank and file will probably come to the ears of the directors sooner or later, but it can take some time, even in our hyper-informed society where things tend to come to light rapidly. In fact, directors are frequently blamed for not being aware of misconduct perpetrated at an organisation on whose governing body they're sitting, even when it's by no means clear how they could have obtained such information or, more importantly, how they could have prevented the errant behaviour. Nevertheless, board directors must of course ensure that their organisation has adequate internal monitoring mechanisms in place to prevent, or discover, any failings or misconduct. I'll come back to this point later. Meanwhile, all these examples show that the core tasks of a governing body and the people who sit on it are not generally well understood. What are board directors supposed to do and what in fact can they do? What added value do they bring to the organisation and to society as a whole?

In addition, the distribution of roles between an organisation's management, board directors and shareholders or partners is not always crystal clear; this can lead to misunderstandings and friction. Once again, the outcome is that the duties which board directors perform vis-à-vis the economy and the wider society are not entirely clear and not properly understood.

In reality, the core duties of the board and the directors sitting on it are not identical in every company or organisation. This is due to differences in the structure of shareholdings, the powers and tasks formally delegated by the shareholders and the tasks devolved to management. Along with other structural factors, these determine the context within which the governing body is required to fulfil its duties. Temporary factors, such as the financial health of the company or organisation, also play a role. I'll come back to all these factors in the next chapter.

Limited liability companies and not-for-profit organisations

For the purposes of this book, whenever I refer to a board of directors, I mean the governing body of either a for-profit company or an enterprise or organisation without profit motive. Companies include: stock-market-listed firms, with or without major shareholders; private limited liability companies whose equity is not traded on the stock market but may be held by various shareholders; and other types of companies which have a genuine governing body. By organisations without profit motive I mean hospitals, cultural associations, educational establishments, social or charitable organisations and the like. These organisations are generally regarded as belonging to the 'non-profit' sector, although they may, and often do, make profits.

In fact, I would argue that the frequently-cited distinction between 'for-profit' and 'non-profit' enterprises is not necessarily the most meaningful one. Belgian law makes a formal distinction between vennootschappen/sociétés, i.e. limited liability companies, and verenigingen/associations — a term which is often translated into English as 'associations' but which carries a specific meaning absent from the normal English sense of an 'association', namely that whereas shareholders in a company have a claim on the profits made and may sell their rights to future profits in the form of shares, no such rights exist for those who set up an 'association' within the meaning of this law, even though it may in fact make profits. Any profits made by such 'associations' must be used to further the 'purpose' or 'object' for which the organisation was set up, and this remains the case even in the event of liquidation.

Having said that, in this book I will nevertheless address the duties and roles of the governing bodies of both types of organisation together. This does not mean that I regard their functions and behaviour as identical, but they do have similar roles. In actual fact, I would argue that all governing bodies, irrespective of the categories into which their organisations may fall, differ somewhat from each other, as they have to operate within differing contexts. You can only really grasp the differences that exist in practice if you shed light on the context in which each given governing body is operating. This is the main subject of Chapter 2 of this book.

The board of directors of a company or organisation is a governing body appointed by the shareholders with the mission of taking all action necessary to fulfil the goal or purpose of the enterprise or organisation. This is, by and large, what is set out in Belgium's legislation governing the organisation and running of 'companies and associations' (see Box above), which was extensively updated as of early 2019 by the Federal Parliament, following a proposal from Justice Minister Koen Geens. For more detail on this new legislation, see the *Belgian Code of Companies and Associations* (BCCA).

We find similar definitions of the tasks and duties of the governing body of a company in other countries. The way these are formulated tends to differ from country to country but the essential point remains the same, namely – to use a short, powerful expression – *"to do everything necessary"*. The formulation will describe what is expected of a board of directors and in what respects the directors are to be held accountable to the shareholders and associates and also to the regulator, the tax authorities and sometimes to certain other 'stakeholders' as well. As the official governing body, the board of directors in principle plays a crucial role in the legal structure of the enterprise (as a for-profit company or not-for-profit organisation) which shapes the activities of the business or organisation.

The four core duties of the governing body

"To do everything necessary" can in practice be broken down into four core duties. By this I don't mean that a board can push to one side the all-embracing responsibility which it has. On the contrary, this is simply an attempt to endow this imperative with some concrete content, i.e. what must a board of directors actually do in order to be able to assume responsibility for everything?

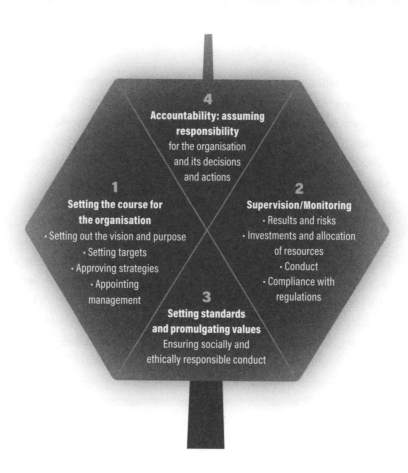

The Duty Diamond

The four core duties of a board of directors

This diagram is a visual representation of the four core duties of a governing body. I call it the Duty Diamond. Just as the various facets of a diamond can reflect a greater or lesser degree of light or draw the viewer's attention to a greater or lesser extent, a particular board may place greater or lesser emphasis on any of the tasks represented. A diamond is also an appropriate reference in that the governing body must always remain connected to the hard core of its duties. I've hung the diamond on a kind of stand that enables it to move freely. It will soon become clear just why this is necessary.

The board of directors is basically there to point the way forward – or set the course – for the company or organisation. However, the extent to which that happens can vary sharply from one board to another. Much depends on the context in which the board is operating. I'll come back to this point in greater detail in Chapter 2. Nevertheless, whether the running of the company is in the hands of the shareholders – which is often the case with family businesses – or entrusted to management, as is common at major listed corporations, the basic aspects of the course-setting task still remain with the board. So in every case, the governing body will act as a sounding board for both shareholders and managers, providing comments and suggestions regarding the direction in which the organisation should be heading.

The difference between decision-making, approving and execution

Confusion sometimes arises over what exactly is meant by decision-making, approving and execution.

Decision-making means that you look at a number of options and select the one that is most conducive to attaining the organisation's targets.

Approving means confirming a choice that has already been made from among a number of options. In practice, this means that if, for instance, the management wants to construct a new storage facility requiring investment exceeding the allocated budget or involve resources above and beyond management's devolved decision-making powers, then they will have to seek the approval of the board, or — in exceptional cases as provided for in the company statutes — of the shareholders. If the board refuses to approve the proposal for a decision, the management will have to come up with a new proposal.

However, things might be done differently: the board might wish to make the decision itself, in which case the management will be tasked to list the options and provide an assessment of each so that the board can decide. This approach is more common at small or family-owned companies, and I've observed that also at not-for-profit organisations it's often the governing body that takes such decisions. At major listed corporations, however, the board will usually confine itself to approving or rejecting management proposals.

Following the decision and its approval, the next step is of course execution – implementing the decision. In practically all cases, it's the management that will be tasked to implement the decision.

If the directors insist too often that initiatives be passed up to board level for decision, this can have a negative effect on the management, who may be discouraged and feel that their professional skills are not being taken seriously. If managers are merely tasked to do the preparatory work for a decision, they may not subsequently be properly motivated to implement it. Conversely, board members may well feel that their true worth is being slighted if they are called upon merely to rubber-stamp decisions taken by management.

In many organisations, the board has a relatively large course-setting role. This doesn't mean that the directors will actually be running the organisation or executing the decisions that have been taken. What it actually means is that they will take a hand in pointing the way forward. How the organisation will proceed along that road and what exactly needs to happen to ensure success will be for the management, under the leadership of the chief executive officer, rather than the directors, to decide. The board may for instance decide that the business should be developing in a more European direction or that part of the production should be transferred over to Asia. The precise manner in which this should

> The board of directors will point the way, but management will decide how exactly to proceed along the path.

be done is however a matter for the executive arm of the company, although, in mapping out the way ahead, the management will of course be expected to stay within the budget already approved – or due to be approved – by the board of directors.

The board of directors usually also has a considerable role to play when it comes to changing the direction in which the enterprise is heading, or rescinding strategic plans that are not proving successful. The board of an investment company that has been endeavouring for several years to make successful investments in a certain technology may decide not to remain in that market any longer if the directors don't believe that the firm has the right talent available to assess and follow through on such investments, or that the ROI is too low or the risks too high. Similarly, the board may decide to cease investing in the development of a new product if the directors conclude that the product development budget has got out of hand and no workable product that meets the stated specifications can be developed.

It's vital that the governing body should be in a position to take a decision to change the strategic direction in which the company is heading, because the management may be inclined to keep pushing ahead with a strategic initiative in spite of an obvious lack of success. This may be because the management have made a wrong assessment of the situation and are reluctant to admit their mistake. Of course, the board may also make a mistake when it comes to assessing the desirability of changing course. This is why it's advisable for directors and managers to hold thorough discussions on a possible change of course. The need for this kind of discussion is one of the fundamental reasons why it's so useful for a company to have a governing body as well as an executive body. Such discussions lead to more thoroughly thought-out decisions about the course which the business or organisation ought to be following.

Mergers and acquisitions will also have a decisive impact on the direction in which an organisation goes and the way in which it's managed. It's therefore hardly surprising that decisions in this area are also an important part of the core duties of a board of directors.

The directors can moreover bring an extra dimension to discussions about mergers and acquisitions. A big part of the discussions will be about the consequences of a takeover operation for strategy, organisation and management. However, there's one financial aspect that will require a great deal of attention: the acquisition price. Though it might seem amazing, the price is not always discussed in depth and with hindsight may often seem too high. There are two possible explanations for this. First and foremost, most of the attention during takeover talks is focused on the strategic aspects of bringing the two businesses together – the markets which the enterprise will be able to conquer after the takeover or merger; the technologies that the firm will be able to access; and the production facilities or raw materials that the company will obtain. A second reason why the acquisition price frequently turns out to be too high is that the expected synergies from the merger may have been overestimated. The proponents of the deal frequently see considerable opportunities to offload existing products on to the customers of the newly-acquired firm, or vice versa. They may also be too quick to assume that large cost savings can be made among the support functions. However, experience has taught me that many of the gains which people expect to achieve through synergies don't actually materialise at the end of the day. You can always calculate this or that on paper, but what turns out in practice is often very different. Synergies require smooth integration between the merging businesses, which is often in practice not achievable due to strong resistance within the two organisations.

Statistical analyses show that many corporate acquisitions are unsuccessful and sometimes even destroy, rather than create, value – clear proof that the top management and the board have given too little thought to the acquisition price. The price and the feasibility of mutual integration following the takeover ought to be key points for consideration by the directors.

Strategists are sometimes too dominant!

Mergers and acquisitions frequently constitute a vital part of a business strategy. Penetrating a foreign market, acquiring a breakthrough technology, strengthening the firm's position in its domestic market, starting a new or complementary activity, or restoring profitability in a given sector - successful acquisitions can make all these things possible and such moves will be part of a company's major strategic planning.

However, the strategic significance of company takeovers stands in stark contrast to the rather modest successes achieved. A number of good academic studies reveal that takeovers rarely deliver the expected result. The majority of acquisitions manage to destroy, rather than create, value. Far from achieving the desirable outcome $1 + 1 = 3$, the equation often works out at less than 2, which must be seen as a serious failure of the company's strategic planning.

The main reason for this is that companies usually pay much too much for their acquisitions. This is good for the shareholders of the company being acquired but bad for the acquiring firm. This probably also explains why the shareholders of Belgian companies that are subject to takeovers are usually - though not always - satisfied with the deal. They're sitting on the right side of the negotiating table. This is a different way of looking at the ongoing debate about how to prevent control over Belgian companies from being transferred abroad. Unfortunately, public opinion sees this the other way round. Value is generally not created but transferred from one shareholder to another. There are dozens of examples of value loss when acquisitions take place.

How does it come about that companies pay too much in order to achieve their strategy through acquisitions? The answer can be found in the governance structures of the companies concerned. Shareholders who are closely involved in the running of a company can take steps to ensure that the firm doesn't make expensive acquisitions. This is only logical, as it's the shareholders who pay the price for the strategy. However, when management is able to act in an unrestrained manner, then no price ticket will seem too expensive to them if it enables them to implement their strategy, and so we tend to see overpriced strategic acquisitions taking place. However, it has long been the case that even large institutional investment funds which hold stakes in companies with acquisition ambitions don't always take care to ensure that they pay an appropriate price for their strategic acquisitions. Even these investors allow themselves to be seduced by the siren song of the strategists, who are prepared to make the acquisition at virtually any price. The fact that institutional investors allow themselves to be carried away like this has, I suppose, to do with their desire to turn small businesses into bigger, more impressive companies, which in turn makes it easier for them to increase the value of their stake. Institutional investors can also be rather capricious: before a takeover, they're in favour, but if it turns out badly they're against it.

So why do directors agree to such overpriced acquisitions? What happens inside the boardroom to prevent projected takeovers being blocked in good time?

I think I can make an informed guess as to what might be going on in the boardroom. I don't doubt that all the directors want the best strategy for the company to prevail. They know that they're accountable to the shareholders. The strategy is presented by the optimists and visionaries using dozens of slides. They will have a lot of support inside the company, as well as among analysts and the general public. The realists on the board look at the expected value creation from the deal and compare that with the acquisition price. This discussion about value creation will not of course be genuinely objective. What additional revenue will we bring in? What margins? What will be the cost of integration? There'll be a lot of estimations about what's likely to happen in the future but no-one can say exactly what will happen. The discussion will be dominated by the strategists and visionaries, who will push the view that "we need to act now – this is a unique opportunity!"

Management gurus might talk about a 'game-changing' moment but this is generally nonsense. Meanwhile, the realists have the feeling that they're being regarded as 'bookkeepers' who haven't an atom of business flair and ambition in them. As a result of the discussion, everything will be re-examined, the financial models will be re-calculated and then, yes, the deal can still work, even at the high acquisition price, especially when you take a very long-term view! This is highly dangerous reasoning. And things get even more desperate if the acquisition price shoots up during the takeover battle. The board will come under strong pressure, along the lines of: "If we give up now we'll lose face, we'll look like losers." In this kind of situation, the struggle between the optimists and the realists is most often won by the optimists. After all, we would all rather be optimistic strategists than realistic accountants.

The approval process for an important investment project also offers the board of directors an opportunity to provide the company or organisation with orientation and leadership. When management comes up with a plan to invest in expanding a production unit on a particular site, this is a good opportunity to think again about the direction in which the firm is going. Does the company really wish to expand on this site? Does it really want to have extra manufacturing capacity for a given product? Should it in fact continue with production activities at all? These are all questions that can legitimately be asked whenever a proposal for investment is tabled, thus placing the company strategy under the microscope once again.

The most important mechanism by which the board of directors can set the course for the company is in its recruitment of a chief executive officer and perhaps also of the rest of the top management. At many companies, it's the board of directors that determines the profile of the management. This is however not always the case; much depends on the context within which the board is operating. I'll discuss this in the next chapter.

By drawing up the desired profile of the CEO and the other members of the executive, the directors will be deciding in an indirect manner on the strategic orientation of the business. If the profile states that the CEO they wish to hire must above all be familiar with the Asian market, this tells you that the board is hoping to expand the business into Asia. If the board is looking for a chief executive who's familiar with digitalisation, that also tells you a lot about their intentions. Conversely, the board might decide to replace the CEO. This usually happens when the directors are unhappy with the results the company is posting, or alternatively the current CEO may not have the right profile or sufficient dynamism, experience or skills to be able to take the firm in a different direction.

However, the director's role cannot be equated with that of a ship's captain. The captain is in charge. He steers the ship and commands the crew. This is not a job for board directors. They can more accurately be compared with the shipowners. They provide the financial resources and decide which ports the ship should sail to. It's then up to the captain to decide which route to take and how to steer the vessel along it.

We can make a useful comparison here with the famous Dutch East India Company, which was founded in the Netherlands in 1602 for the purpose of sending ships to India and other destinations in Asia in order to acquire and trade in spices. The Company, widely known by its Dutch abbreviation VOC, was directed by a 17-man body known as 'The Seventeen', who raised the capital for each voyage and appointed a captain and crew to make the expedition.[4] The Seventeen commissioned the expedition, but once the ship had put out to sea, the captain was in command and they had to wait patiently until the vessel returned home. Incidentally, it's quite probable that the VOC's 'Seventeen' were the first ever board of directors in business history.

---

4 See Femme S. Gaastra – *De geschiedenis van de Verenigde Oost-Indische Companie of VOC. [The History of the United East India Company (VOC)].* Zutphen: Walburg Pers, 2002, especially Chapters 1 and 5. The actual governance structure was somewhat more complex than the simplified version I'm using here.

SUPERVISION AND MONITORING

The core duty of a board of directors that's most widely recognised, certainly more so than the course-setting function, is its role in providing oversight, supervision and monitoring. The business operates with resources that have mainly been raised from shareholders and financiers. Those shareholders and financiers count on the directors to exercise supervision as regards how those resources are used.

The financial, legal and corporate governance literature highlights a problem that can arise whenever someone provides resources to another person with a view to jointly carrying out a project: this is known as the 'agency problem'. The agency problem arises because the principal – the money provider – is unable to assess immediately whether the money is being used properly by the agent. If the intended result is not achieved, the principal doesn't really know whether this is due to unfortunate circumstances or misuse of the resources by the agent. The principal might see misuse in the agent's actions because the interests of the two parties are not perfectly aligned: any appropriations made by the agent are basically coming out of the pocket of the principal.

We find the agency problem whenever a company or organisation uses resources provided by shareholders and financiers, because the suppliers of funds are never quite sure that their money is being used for the intended purpose. The supervisory and monitoring role of the governing body therefore consists of taking steps to ensure that the funds are used properly and that the agency problem doesn't arise. It's clear however that the mere existence of a board of directors won't always necessarily obviate the agency problem. The directors cannot control every aspect and, moreover, directors who don't themselves have any shareholding in the firm won't suffer any financial disadvantage if funds are misused by the management. Directors might even conspire with the management to misappropriate shareholders' money.

To avoid the board members themselves becoming part of the agency problem, various measures are generally taken to discourage them from threatening the interests of the shareholders or sponsors and encourage each of them to build a reputation as a credible, trustworthy director. There are basically three types of measures designed to ensure that directors carry out their supervisory and monitoring duties in a proper manner.

The first type of measure is legal. Submitting falsified annual accounts is a criminal offence which remains punishable for a good many years after the fact. Providing shareholders with false or misleading information is also a criminal act. These legal provisions don't entirely solve the agency problem but they do at least make misuse of funds punishable by law.

The second type of measure consists of providing the governing body with extra tools for monitoring the use of company resources. The board is required to commission external auditors to check the accounts several times a year so as to ensure that they're presenting a fair picture of how the resources are being used. Furthermore, it's mandatory for listed firms to set up an audit committee, consisting of a number of board directors who are given the task of maintaining oversight over the accounts and also over the work of the external auditors. If it should become apparent that the relationship between the management and the external auditors has become too close to ensure objective supervision, the audit committee is supposed to argue for the appointment of a different auditing firm when the existing auditors' mandate expires. When a company is taken over, the directors of the acquiring firm often demand the appointment of a new auditor so as to obtain an objective view of the results and current resources of the new acquisition.

In addition to the external auditors, companies usually have one or more internal auditors reporting to management and the board. Their job is to keep management and the members of the audit committee informed about the use made of funds and resources, spot any fraudulent practice, and make recommendations for improvements designed to ensure more efficient use of resources. A separate unit may also be set up to handle fraud prevention and detection.

There's also a third way to make it less likely that board members will fail in their duty to maintain supervision over the use of company resources: appointing directors with a strong reputation for integrity and trustworthiness. There are two reasons for doing so. First and foremost, such people will probably have the skills to be able to exercise effective supervision. They'll know where they ought to be looking. But there's a second reason. If those directors discover during their tenure of a board seat that company resources are being used in an inappropriate manner then they'll do everything in their power to avoid reputational damage. So it's very much in their interest to ensure that the business is properly supervised. Any damage to a director's reputation, trustworthiness or integrity will affect not only his/her personal standing but also his/her market value.

> **Any damage to a director's reputation will affect his/her personal standing and market value.**

So how can board members exercise supervision over the use of the funds provided by shareholders and financiers? In addition to the task of appointing auditors, the process of approving the company budget is a powerful *ex ante* tool to help keep a grip on the allocation of resources before any money is actually spent. An *ex post* comparison of the budget with the results posted, i.e. after the funds have been spent, is also an excellent way to judge whether the management is using those funds properly and making an effort to achieve the maximum with the available resources. If management tables a budget showing a large deficit, this might be a sign that the firm doesn't have the means to achieve all its plans and that choices need to be made, or perhaps that the organisation is in a transition phase. In that case, consideration will have to be given to whether the deficit budget can be financed and whether this will lead to a real transformation of the company going forward.

The budget process doesn't only have a supervisory or monitoring purpose. It's also a way for directors to see whether the company or organisation is still on course as agreed with the board. The budget discussion is therefore a very important point on the agenda, which provides the governing body with the opportunity to pursue three aspects of its core duties: to verify that the organisation is moving in the desired direction and investing accordingly; to assess the quality of the management; and to ascertain whether the resources provided are being used properly.

Supervision and monitoring are of course not only about the use of resources. The board will also keep an eye on the results posted and the risks that the enterprise runs in the course of its activities. In assessing the results, the board will have recourse to the company accounts, which they will of course have to approve before they're made public. The fact that this approval is required creates an extra stimulus for the directors to examine the accounts carefully: they will bear the responsibility if the stated results are later found to be incorrect. Examining the accounts showing the results also provides an opportunity to benchmark the company's performance – i.e. to compare it with similar businesses. If it appears that the enterprise is doing worse than its competitors, that will be a good starting point for the directors to investigate, i.e. ask questions about the strategy pursued by the company, the effectiveness of the management, about efficiency and productivity, and judge whether there has been any waste of resources.

Apart from examining performance, there is an increasing imperative at banks and other types of companies to monitor and assess risk. This is definitely one of the board's most important supervisory tasks. The difficulty here however is that very few standard yardsticks exist for measuring risk. Risk analysis is very often conducted in an ad hoc manner that differs from company to company. These days, we often hear about the 'risk appetite' of a company or financial institution. This is a fine concept, but it's very hard to standardise, and every company tends to take a different approach when measuring it, which makes it difficult for directors to fulfil their duty in this area. The lack of standardisation is due to the fact that risks may arise at any moment in any area of the organisation. The company share price risk on the stock market is quite easy to express and measure, but within the company, there is no such standard measurement to hand.

Monitoring the company results and the risks that the business is running is an entirely different matter than exercising supervision over the use of resources. How can the board ensure that the management and workforce conduct themselves as expected? How can the firm try to ensure that the products sold to the customers perfectly meet their requirements? How can you guarantee that the products are safe or that company employees have a safe environment in which to work, that energy is being used economically, or that price collusion with competitors isn't happening? So, if you're a company director, there'll be dozens of areas of management or workforce behaviour that you will in principle need to keep an eye on, in order to ensure that the conduct of the company as a whole is blameless. Maintaining such widespread surveillance is an almost impossible task. Nevertheless, there are two ways in which directors can endeavour to do so. The first is by laying down some basic principles for running the business – otherwise known as company policies. Depending on the type of company, you can draw up policies on safety, energy consumption, product sales, contacts with competitors, and so on. The initiative here will come from the management: they're the ones to draw up the policies. However, the board of directors will have to approve those policies, and in so doing may decide to adjust them. It is of course preferable that the governing body determines such policies, after which the internal auditors or Compliance managers should be able to monitor their application.

A second way for the governing body to maintain oversight over conduct across the organisation is to ensure the prevalence of a particular corporate culture. Once again, it will not be the board that implements the corporate culture, but the directors can ensure that the management takes the necessary steps. Moreover, directors can set an example with their own conduct. Nothing is so detrimental to corporate culture and conduct within an organisation as the perception that the people at the top can do whatever they like while those working in the rest of the organisation are expected to conduct themselves in a responsible manner.

SETTING STANDARDS AND PROMULGATING VALUES

This constitutes the third of a governing body's core duties. The board of directors has the task of establishing core values and standards according to which the organisation is expected to operate. In actual fact, the board's duty consists of ensuring that the hands-on management team draws up a set of standards and values for themselves and the workforce. The directors then have responsibility for approving those values and standards and ensuring that everyone – including themselves – lives up to them. Most often, a corporate values statement will be drawn up. Once the board has approved the statement, those values usually take on greater coercive force and it will then be much harder for management to disregard them or turn a blind eye to undesirable conduct in specific cases. Some very concrete questions can be addressed in this kind of corporate values statement, such as for instance: are managers who hold company shares or warrants entitled to trade these securities on the stock market? Or: how are insiders expected to treat information entrusted to them by the company?

When people talk about a corporate values statement, most of them immediately think of ethical standards. However, I think we need to look at things more broadly. In today's world, any enterprise needs to draw up a statement setting out its intention to behave in

> The directors are responsible for approving the corporate values and standards and ensuring that people at the company – including themselves – live up to them.

a sustainable and socially responsible manner towards its customers, suppliers, employees, the environment and the region(s) where the company operates and does business. Nowadays a company

Shareholders nowadays don't let companies get away with shirking their social responsibilities.

or organisation cannot afford to simply take no notice of the impact it has on the people who are, directly or indirectly, affected by its actions, and on the environment. There are plenty of recent examples – take for instance Volkswagen 'fiddling' its engine emissions data, which I'll come back to later in this book – which show how companies that neglect their role in society may be punished by their shareholders and see their share price fall sharply. The governing body of a company or organisation therefore needs to ensure that the management are attentive to its social responsibilities – not just paying lip service to a major social trend, but realising that nowadays this is part and parcel of running a company. And it's not only the general public who have this expectation but increasingly shareholders as well – a point that's often overlooked.

A corporate values statement can also draw attention to the importance of promoting an inclusive society, in which there is diversity and respectful behaviour. The directors can certainly impress it upon the management that they need to pay attention to all these aspects. They can even make management responsible for them.

As well as soft values, the corporate values statement may also put forward harder values. Companies ought to regard initiative, innovation and entrepreneurial spirit as crucial values and encourage their employees to act along these lines. You then also need to encourage the management to follow through on the consequences of this thinking. If the management don't want employees to take their own initiatives there's no sense in including concepts such as entrepreneurship and innovation in the statement.

Even where the management acts on its own initiative to issue strong, but balanced, statements and declarations regarding the company's standards and values, the directors should still support those

If you trample your own
values underfoot, what
can you expect from your
employees?

initiatives and help bring them to fruition.
Once again, the basic principle holds good:
if the top people don't behave in accordance
with the corporate standards and values,
the employees won't give any credence to
the overall approach. And then socially responsible conduct simply
won't take hold in the company.

ACCOUNTABILITY

The directors have a collective duty to do everything necessary to steer
the company, maintain supervision and monitor what happens at the
firm. If something goes wrong, they can in fact be held liable, so it's
very much in their interest to ensure that everything runs as it should.
In many cases, directors take out liability insurance to cover such an
eventuality and will use the insured sum for their legal defence if they
are accused of administrative errors or negligence.

Directors are always very concerned about potential liabilities – and
rightly so. However, it's very rare that a board member is actually
found guilty of wrongdoing. This has of course led to some cynical
remarks in the press and among public opinion, alleging the existence
of a 'class justice' system that protects company directors. Personally,
I think that the small number of such criminal convictions has less
to do with 'class justice' than the fact that it's extremely difficult to
prove a direct causal link between a decision that was taken or not
taken and the consequences as regards the behaviour, results or values of the corporation. This is somewhat easier when the charge is
linked to financial information, where for instance investors and other
stakeholders have been misled regarding the value of the company's
results, assets or liabilities. This often becomes very important in the
event of a capital increase. However, a simple failure on the part of
the directors to reveal in a timely fashion any information likely to
influence the company's value will sometimes lead to legal claims.

The board of directors is in principle also responsible for any agreements or commitments that the company or organisation enters into with parties with whom it works. In practice, the board will invariably delegate such powers to the chief executive or managing director, or other company personnel, who will then act on behalf of the company or board of directors. In the case of very important commitments, a statement must be formally recorded in the minutes of the board meeting to the effect that the directors have indeed given their approval for the management to conclude the agreement or commitment. The board minutes therefore constitute an extremely important document. Firstly, they prove that the meeting in question actually took place; secondly, they provide an accurate record of the decisions taken (or at least this should be the case); and thirdly they can be used to show third parties exactly how the meeting went and how the discussions were conducted.

Company directors also bear responsibility for the obligations and requirements imposed by law or supervisory authorities. The relevant documents will be drawn up by management but, in most cases, they can be submitted to the authorities only after they have been signed off by the board.

* * *

In the preceding pages I've set out all the core duties of a board of directors. However, it's important to point out that different governing bodies go about fulfilling these duties in different ways. Some boards place greater emphasis on supervision and monitoring and devote less attention to setting the course for the organisation. You can also find boards that do things the other way round. Governing bodies can in practice differ considerably from one another in this area. However, most boards approach the third and fourth of their core duties – setting standards and promulgating values, and assuming responsibility – in a very similar way.

Various kinds of governing bodies

Figure 2 below sets out the various kinds of governing bodies in a simplified schema. Some boards devote more attention than others to supervisory tasks. These are shown in the bottom left section of the triangle. Other boards are more closely involved in setting the course for the company or organisation and tend to take a more executive approach. These are placed in the bottom right section. In the top section of the triangle, I've placed governing bodies that can be described as 'entrepreneurial'. An entrepreneurial board will involve itself closely in strategic matters, such as putting forward new initiatives and suggesting concrete ways of bringing them to fruition. In my experience, such entrepreneurial boards are mainly to be found in new technology startups financed by venture capitalists. In these cases, the directors are mostly seasoned technology investors or serial entrepreneurs who have already set up several companies and have lots of experience in starting up and growing a business. I've seen similar situations with some family firms, where family members who are closely involved in the enterprise approach the work of the board of directors in an entrepreneurial manner.

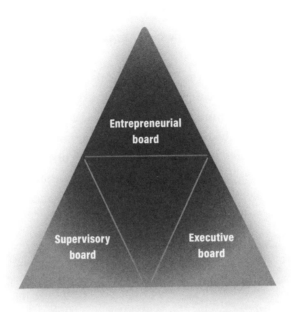

Entrepreneurial
board

Supervisory
board

Executive
board

The various kinds of boards

Figure 3 below illustrates how a board of directors that's more geared to course-setting differs from a board which takes a more supervisory approach. Basically, our original Duty Diamond has been tilted to the left (a governing body with a more course-setting approach) or the right (weighted towards a more supervisory role). The other roles haven't disappeared but the emphasis is definitely on either the course-setting or the supervisory aspect of the board's work.

A ONE-TIER VERSUS TWO-TIER APPROACH

In some countries, such as Germany and the Netherlands, the legislators have made formal provision for entrusting the core duties of
supervision/monitoring on the one hand and course-setting on the
other two distinct bodies. Accordingly, a governing body known as
the *Raad van Commissarissen* (literally: Council of Commissioners)
came into being in the Netherlands, and a similar body called the
Aufsichtsrat (literally: Oversight Council), which is almost exclusively

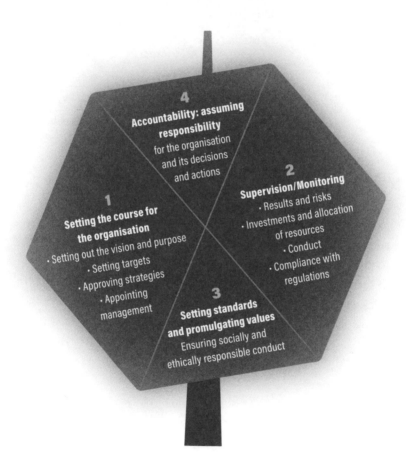

4
Accountability: assuming responsibility
for the organisation
and its decisions
and actions

1
Setting the course for the organisation
· Setting out the vision and purpose
· Setting targets
· Approving strategies
· Appointing management

2
Supervision/Monitoring
· Results and risks
· Investments and allocation of resources
· Conduct
· Compliance with regulations

3
Setting standards and promulgating values
Ensuring socially and
ethically responsible conduct

The board takes a more 'course-setting' approach

confined to the supervisory role, was introduced in Germany. These bodies are not empowered to set the course which the company is expected to follow, apart from the fact that they have the task of appointing the members of the executive board. In Germany, this executive board bears the name *Vorstand* (derived from a verb meaning to lead, head up or preside) and in the Netherlands is called the *Raad van Bestuur* (literally Management Council).[5] We therefore see twin governance bodies – generally known as a 'two-tier board' – operating in those countries.

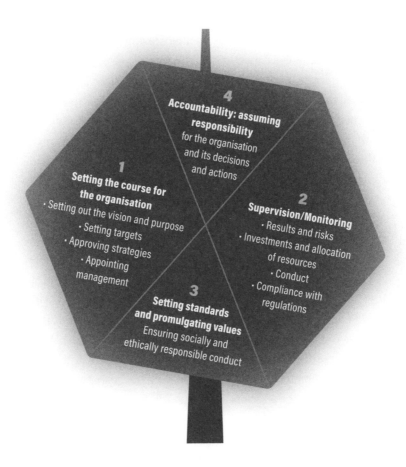

The directors will have a more 'supervisory' role

Meanwhile, in the English-speaking countries and much of Europe, companies are still supervised by a 'one-tier' board tasked to carry out both of the two main core duties. Over the years there has been a great deal of discussion in Belgium about the pros and cons of the two systems of corporate governance, and recently-enacted legislation in principle gives shareholders a choice between one-tier and two-tier governance. It will be very interesting to see which Belgian firms opt for which system and what benefits – in terms of governance – they're able to draw from their chosen approach. The Netherlands already passed legislation back in 2013 giving companies a free choice between the two governance models, so corporate structures in these two neighbouring countries may well be moving closer together.

Banking sector legislation in Belgium in any case requires Belgian banks to operate under a two-tier system. Banks have an executive board, all members of which also sit on the board of directors, which has a mainly supervisory role. However, the separation of functions between the executive and supervisory boards is not entirely clear-cut, as the board of directors will express its views upfront on very significant, or potentially risky, investments. Moreover, there seems now to be a tendency among both national and European regulators to seek to involve the board of directors more closely in the actual running of the bank, shrinking the gap between the governing and executive bodies, especially in the fields of risk management and remuneration.

The advantage of a two-tier system is that the fulfilment of the directors' supervision and monitoring duties is not hindered by the need to set the course for the organisation and that each of these two core duties can therefore be carried out in a more independent manner. One disadvantage is that this approach tends to distance the supervisory/monitoring body somewhat from the business, making it more difficult for the directors to keep up with what's really happening inside the company.

---

5 Confusingly, the title *Raad van Bestuur* is used in Belgium in a different sense, signifying the (one-tier) Board of Directors.

To sum up

Significant differences exist in the way different governing bodies carry out their core duties. This means that boards may differ widely from one to another, so we can accurately say that there actually exist different types of corporate governance bodies. I would even go so far as to say that any given board will differ from all others. The reason why such differences exist between corporate governance bodies is that they often have to operate in different contexts and under different circumstances. These variations in context and how they affect directors' core duties are the subject of my next chapter.

CHAPTER 2

One board is not the same as another

The importance of context

A board of directors has four core duties, which were described in the previous chapter. However, different boards don't carry out those duties in exactly the same way and don't all devote the same amount of energy to all of them. This is because the context in which the boards are operating varies considerably. Consequently, we're justified in saying that there exist various different types of corporate governance bodies. In this chapter, we'll delve deeper into the question of context.

IN MY EXPERIENCE THERE ARE AT LEAST SEVEN STRUCTURAL FACTORS which help to determine how a board of directors carries out its duties: the shareholder structure; the distribution of powers between the general meeting of shareholders (AGM) and the board; the composition of the board; the governance model being used; the powers that are delegated to management; the legislation and regulations in force; and the personal characteristics of the shareholders, board members and managers involved. In addition to these structural elements, there are sometimes temporary factors that help to determine the precise tasks of the board of directors. For instance, the tasks facing the board of a company going through a financial or business crisis or undergoing a fundamental transformation as a result of commercial or techno-logical disruption will be rather different from when a company is performing well and is financially sound and stable.

The various factors represented here are of course not independent of each other. One factor will influence another. For instance, it's obvious that the shareholder structure will affect the way powers are shared between the general meeting of shareholders and the board of directors, and the corporate governance model being used will have a direct impact on the kind of responsibilities that are delegated to the management. In the following pages, I'll address in detail this interaction between the various factors.

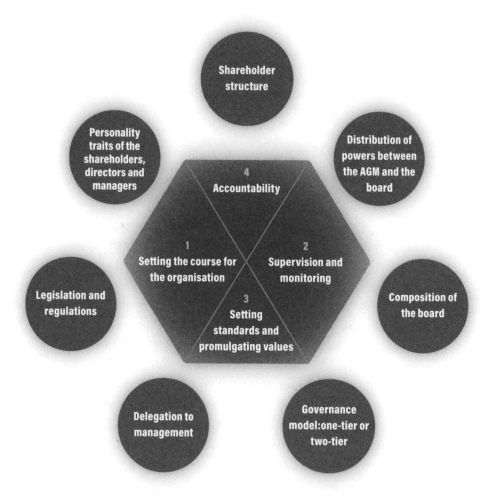

The seven factors which make up the context that
determines the precise duties of a board of directors

Factor 1 Shareholder structure

It would not be useful to set out here all the extensive definitions
of what I mean by terms such as shareholder structure, corporate
governance model, etc. Instead, I'll restrict myself to short descriptions. By shareholder structure, I mean, *inter alia*, the total number
of shareholders, the types of shareholders the company has and

the sharing of powers between them. Are there a large number of shareholders or just a few? Do some shareholders have a relatively large packet of shares or is the stock broadly fragmented? Are the shareholders private investors, investment funds or professional investors, families or perhaps even the state? These various types of shareholder and the balance of power between them make quite a difference as regards the directors' tasks and consequently as regards the way the board works.

SHAREHOLDERS

Limited liability companies have shareholders. Shareholders have rights to any profits distributed by the company and to the value of the company upon sale or liquidation, after all debts and obligations have been settled. The value of a company may rise or fall and there may or may not be distributable profits. There is consequently no guarantee that shareholders will recover their initial investment. The risk inherent in the company is therefore borne by the shareholders. They stand as guarantors that all parties who have claims on the company's assets or revenues will be paid. Any surplus is then for them. However, if there's a shortfall, they don't have to come up with any extra. In principle, the company will declare bankruptcy. A shareholder's liability is limited to the sum s/he paid for his/her stake in the business.

Shareholders don't necessarily have to be real people like Peter, Paul and Mary. Increasingly, company shareholders, whether or not the firm is listed on the stock exchange, are themselves companies. Sometimes these are actually operational companies but most often they're specialist investment entities such as holding companies, investment funds, pension funds, private equity or venture capital firms, or entities set up by families or individual persons to manage their stake in the company. Investment funds and pension funds deserve special attention. They collect capital from private or institutional savers and invest it in all kinds of securities, including equity (company shares). They usually follow a global investment strategy.

With the progressive 'institutionalisation' of shareholdership in Belgium and all Western countries, the relationship between the shareholders and the board of directors has changed radically. Nowadays, directors who come into contact with this sort of shareholder are no longer talking to a person who's investing his/her own money but to a professional asset manager. These managers look at risk, return and the relationship with other corporate equity in the portfolio which they manage and they're in a much better position to make comparisons. They know how foreign telecoms firms are performing and when a biotech company is about to launch a new wonder drug. Moreover, when the company's looking for a new CEO, a new board chair, new directors or managers, institutional investors won't necessarily be content with a local search but will want to search internationally. They'll usually urge the company to seek out the best man or woman for that top job, wherever s/he might currently be.

It's therefore no surprise that board members and managers at listed Belgian companies have become more international in recent years. The 'institutionalisation' of shareholdership is consequently having a direct impact on directors' duties. Moreover, these new kinds of shareholders aren't necessarily prepared to enter into discussion about company strategy. Instead, they often choose to keep their freedom of decision and will perhaps reduce their stake in the firm. To use a current expression, they often choose exit over voice, i.e. they opt to sell off their holding rather than stay and put forward their opinions about what the company ought to be doing. This means that boards have had to learn to live with a fluid shareholder community and to keep a close eye on the company share price, because abnormal upward or downward movements in the price also provide signals as to what shareholders think of the company.

Shareholders often choose exit over voice.

The fact that shareholders risk losing their stake in the firm gives them some basic rights. They can exercise these rights through the mechanism of the company's annual general meetings (AGMs) or extraordinary general meetings (EGMs).

These shareholder gatherings are important events for the board of directors, although I've also discovered that directors often tend to underestimate their importance. It is nevertheless at these gatherings that decisions can be taken on the appointment, remuneration or even dismissal of directors. Shareholders may also ask questions about the company's policies or results. They're called upon to approve – or reject – the annual accounts and the dividend proposed by the board and to grant formal discharge to the directors for the performance of their duties.

These decisions might seem like pure formalities but they're nevertheless essential to the workings of the company and the duties incumbent on board members. Every good company director knows that an active AGM provides a wealth of information about what the more closely involved shareholders think of the company. Especially if the business gets into difficulties, the AGM has a vital role to play. Highly charged examples that one might cite include the Fortis EGM called in January 2009 to approve the sale of the bank to the European BNP Paribas banking group, and the discussion that took place about the takeover of Société Générale de Belgique by the France-based Suez group in 1988. Those were really tumultuous meetings. General meetings of shareholders have very rarely been conducted in such a fashion. However, a meeting doesn't have to be tumultuous in order to be exciting. Different blocks of shareholders sometimes face off against each other and wrangle over the appointment of directors and the remuneration they are to be paid. Activists may use their right to speak at the AGM to take the management to task over the policies being pursued by the company. This happened for instance at the technology firm Barco, whose management came under fire from pacifist movements from about 1997 to 2007 with sharp questions about the company's alleged military activities. I certainly learned from those AGMs that companies need to take account of public opinion and pay close attention to what their shareholders think.

Vocal shareholders

Apart from some small hiccups here and there, AGMs in Belgium are generally rather placid. People listen politely, a few questions – some of them quite pertinent – are asked and the accounts, directors' discharge, and appointments are usually quickly approved. Major shareholder uprisings like those seen at the Fortis meetings in late 2008 and early 2009 are somewhat exceptional. In other countries as well, company AGMs are usually very civilised events. The management talks, the shareholders listen, a few of the more assertive ones ask questions and after the votes are taken the – more or less satisfied – shareholders have a drink.

However, sometimes it seems as if a revolt is breaking out. The shareholders vote down the top managers' pay packet or refuse to approve the re-appointment of several directors. Is this the start of a fruitful debate between shareholders, directors and managers? Should it be and can it be?

Contrary to what a lot of people think, listed companies are organisations that provide opportunities for quite a lot of participation. If you wish to become a company shareholder, you can buy one or more shares for a few dozen euro, put your name on the shareholder register and then stroll into the AGM. There you can ask any questions you wish and keep talking for as long as you like. The chair must allow you to speak, as long as you don't repeat yourself or demand information that might damage the company's business prospects. I know of very few organisations in modern society where you can do this. Some shareholders make considerable use of this right but they're usually the exceptions. These are very often activist groups, which proves once again that it is indeed possible to have your say in a listed company. I must honestly admit that such interventions don't always result in changes to company policy but people can at least express their criticism.

In fact, the AGM can become a forum where shareholders, board members and managers can talk about the workings of the company, its strategy, finances and risks, plus also of course about the remuneration of the top people. It's probably the best place to discuss these subjects.

However, I still come across company bosses who don't think the AGM is very useful and prefer to get it over with as quickly as possible. This is also evident from the fact that directors are often absent from the meeting, though I do have the impression that this has begun to improve in recent years. The reasons why AGMs are not very popular are quite complicated. Important shareholders have other channels through which they can talk to directors. Institutional shareholders often prefer not to speak openly, due to legal considerations, and will confine themselves to casting their vote for or against the proposal on the table. Meanwhile the smaller shareholders, with one or two honourable exceptions, seldom possess the knowledge to ask searching questions. But there's more to it than that. Strategy decisions, designating and appraising the management team, and monitoring the use of company resources are not things which can be done at a public meeting. That's what the board of directors is for. Shareholders can ask questions, call the top people to account, and will need to give or withhold their approval of decisions and actions, but they're not equipped to set the course for the company. The challenge is to enable the various corporate bodies to carry out their specific tasks effectively. I'm firmly convinced that shareholders have a vital role to play at the AGM in ensuring that the company is run properly.

It's essential for a company to have assertive shareholders. But how can you achieve this aim? Modern communication channels can help. More and better contact between the board and the shareholders, together with, or separately from, the management, can be useful. However, recent experience appears to show that no benefits accrue from holding extra meetings between directors and shareholders. This brings the key point to the surface: shareholders must be prepared to take responsibility themselves and, I would argue, they have an obligation to be vocal.

Shareholders in listed companies can of course make their position clear by buying or selling the company's shares, thus causing the share price to rise or fall and sending a signal to the board and the management about what the shareholders want. This kind of signal can sometimes be very meaningful. A falling share price means that the cost of capital will rise, which indicates that the company, with its current management and strategy, is not encouraged to go ahead with new investments. Very often however, stock market signals are too vague to serve as a practical guide for board decisions such as share options for the management, their compensation packages, or even dividend distribution. A good discussion between directors and shareholders can bring clarity to the situation much more quickly.

I'm aware that other ideas are now being put forward with the aim of giving a new dimension to the AGM. Some people would like to turn it into a sort of stakeholders' meeting. I don't go along with this because it will lead to endless palaver and then essential decisions about the running of the company that need to be taken are likely to be squeezed out. This sort of stakeholder consultation can be useful for specific issues but it should instead be conducted in ad hoc meetings.

Extraordinary general meetings (EGMs) are called to decide on changes to the company statutes and also, if the statutes so require, to agree on important strategic decisions such as investments, divestments, and the liquidation of the company.

The attendance at a general meeting of shareholders very rarely shows a representative sample of the company's shareholders. This is at least certainly the case with listed companies. As a rule, it's the same shareholders who put in an appearance year after year at the AGM. This may have something to do with the fact that the attendees are treated to a tasty snack and a nice drink. Investment funds often either stay away, or don't take part in the vote because they think it's more efficient to cast their vote in writing through the intermediary of a specialist service provider. Sometimes it's regrettable that the big investment funds remain so distant from the proceedings. This makes it harder for the board of directors to keep in touch with these important shareholders, there's very little discussion with them, and decision-making at the AGM becomes purely a matter of voting for or against the resolutions put forward. Consequently, a trend develops whereby shareholders become less closely involved with the company, and its equity becomes purely an investment product.

Nevertheless, a good atmosphere generally prevails at the AGM. Now and then tensions arise in the room but the directors shouldn't let themselves get too seriously carried away by the mood among the attendees. At the end of the day, what counts is how the vote on the motion goes. I've seen instances where shareholders have reacted sharply to a proposal, but when the vote was finally taken the vocal dissatisfied ones found themselves very much in the minority. Alternatively, the opposite may happen. People in the room might be singing the praises of a certain nominee for a board seat, but when the votes are counted you find that s/he has barely scraped the required majority. Even the media sometimes allow themselves

A noisy AGM? Only the vote tally really counts.

to be misled by critical questions put at an AGM. However, just because a few shareholders ask pointed questions or the meeting turns noisy that doesn't necessarily mean that there's a real problem. As I just underlined, the only thing that counts for the board of directors is how the vote goes. Was the motion approved or rejected? An obvious comparison can be made with a national Parliament or Congress. The government or administration doesn't find itself in difficulty every time the opposition tables a motion that fails to obtain a majority. The same principle holds good for company shareholder meetings, although – as I pointed out above – good directors know that it's always wise to take notice of any dissatisfaction among the shareholders.

Obviously, if the board is doing its job properly, it will be alert to any reactions from the shareholders. Now and again I hear or sense a certain contempt for the AGM or EGM among directors, who regard these meetings as inexpert gatherings that are largely a waste of time. I think this view is wrong. One shouldn't underestimate how important these sessions are in helping the board of directors to do its job. Moreover, we should of course never forget that by turning up every year at the AGM, the hard-core shareholders are demonstrating their devotion to the enterprise and seeking to fulfil their duty to the company. I often observe this serious attitude in the thorough way shareholders study the meeting documents and ask questions about them, even though those questions may not always be very profound or well-thought-out.

STOCK ANALYSTS AND INVESTOR BEHAVIOUR

Meetings with shareholders don't constitute the only lines of influence brought to bear on the board of directors at a company listed on the stock exchange. Directors must also be attentive to what analysts write about the company's strategy, results and share price movements. Increasing numbers of shareholders nowadays base their investment decisions on analysts' reports. You often hear groans in the boardroom whenever an analyst publishes a report and the directors feel that (yet again!) s/he hasn't quite 'got it'. Here again, it's wise for the directors to listen to what the analyst is saying and read what s/he's written because this is often a sign that the company's financial communication is far from perfect. Furthermore, the analyst's opinion will often be a precursor of investors' views.

In Belgium, another problem arises. First of all, the national stock market is relatively small. Secondly, there are a number of smaller listed firms that still have a good many long-term shareholders who have absolutely no intention of selling their stake in the business, a situation that is known in technical parlance as a 'limited free float'. So daily trading volumes in some equities on the Brussels stock exchange are extremely small, resulting in a shortage of liquidity in particular shares, which in turn means that it just isn't profitable for stockbrokers to have their analysts draw up reports on the equity of smaller companies. Given the limited resources available, the analysts are not always top-quality and – given that they often have insufficient access to all kinds of sector information that might be important when assessing a company – the same goes for their reports. It goes without saying that stockbrokers are more likely to ignore the cost and hire the best analysts if they're able to execute plenty of big trades – which is the case with AB InBev or Solvay equity, rather than for instance Gimv shares.

Why should the board care about this? Because if hardly any analysts are reporting on your firm, it's much harder to get your information across to current or potential shareholders, which could have the effect of depressing the company's stock or making the share price more unstable and unpredictable. Any unforeseen incident may then have a greater impact on the share price because investors are simply not able to accurately assess the consequences of the incident. Moreover, if very few analysts are rating your stock and they're all local, foreign investors are unlikely to get to know much about your company and it will then be difficult to build a more international shareholdership, which will in turn make it harder for the directors to attract more capital to the business. All this puts an even greater burden on the management and board of directors to keep the shareholders well informed.

PROXY ADVISORS

Shareholders are expected to attend the AGMs and EGMs and vote on the proposals tabled by the board, including directors' discharge, new appointments, dividend distribution and capital reduction, to name but a few. Over the last few years, we've seen the rise of 'proxy advisory service' specialists that provide shareholders in listed companies with recommendations on how they should cast their votes. There's clearly a need for this type of corporate governance advisor. International investors may have stakes in dozens of companies in as many countries, with different languages, legislation and customs, so they will obviously need advisors who can formulate recommendations on how to vote their shares. This tends to upset directors when those recommendations go against what the board is proposing. Shareholders are sometimes advised to reject the appointment of directors or managers or to give the thumbs down to proposed changes to the company statutes. Directors certainly don't appreciate this kind of proxy advisor recommendations, to put it mildly.

> Directors tend to get upset when shareholders follow the recommendations of proxy advisors.

Sometimes the directors are right. It's not always easy to understand what the voting recommendations are based on, so it can be hard to hold a coherent discussion about them. I've seen at least one instance where such voting advice was clearly illogical. All the proposals for statute changes were given a positive recommendation but shareholders were nevertheless advised to reject the motion to delegate to management the task of adapting the statutes, which ought to have been a mere formality. However, proxy advisors are now a reality which directors would be wise to take into account when drafting proposals for the AGM, if they wish to avoid a nasty situation where a resolution that they table is rejected by a large group of shareholders.

In fact, a number of large international investment funds have actually undertaken to always follow the voting recommendations given by their proxy advisors. Sometimes I wonder whether investors who follow this kind of policy are really fulfilling their shareholder duties properly. Shouldn't we expect every shareholder to form an entirely independent opinion on the board's proposals? Is blindly following the advice of a third party really compatible with the need for every shareholder to form an independent, considered opinion?

FAMILIES WITH TIGHT CONTROL

When a family holds a large equity stake – whether we're talking about a listed firm or an unlisted business – there's often a close bond between the shareholders and the company, with family members sometimes, for instance, working as CEO or managers. This situation is rarely an easy one for board members, who can find themselves between a rock and a hard place. On the one hand, the directors need to monitor managers' performance and may conclude that the current management is inadequate to the task. On the other hand, they have to take account of the wishes of the shareholders. In theory, it's quite easy to resolve this conflict: the board must simply choose whatever is best for the business. However, it's not always possible to figure out in an objective and scientific way what is best for the business. The principles of business economics and business administration cannot accurately predict what the best decisions for the enterprise will turn out to be. Company results depend not only on managerial competence but also on circumstances and luck. This sort of situation calls for considerable diplomacy on the part of the directors.

This situation becomes even more complex if the family is made up of various different branches or if a number of families hold stakes in the company. Intra-family friction can rapidly increase if the company's performance starts to slip and members of one or other branch of the family are – or might be – responsible. Any director who has no feel for this kind of complexity or lacks emotional intelligence is not likely to achieve much here. I'm certainly not trying to suggest that board members should slavishly follow the wishes and demands of the family. On the contrary! But they do need to find a way to keep the business on the right track. It can sometimes help directors to bear in mind the other employees working at the company, who also have families. If you allow a business to go under due to a family feud, other unrelated families will be affected as well. Therefore, the best thing the directors can do at any time is to keep on striving to do what is best for the company.

In the foregoing pages, I've consistently used the term 'company shareholders'. But aren't the shareholders in fact the owners? It all depends on how you define 'ownership'. If you mean that the shareholder owns his or her share in the profits or the value of the company, then there's no doubt about it. But a shareholder in a company, whether or not it's listed on the stock exchange, does not own the firm's assets and liabilities or all its future revenue streams. These belong to a legal person, which is the company itself. Responsibility for setting the course for the company and growing its balance sheet and revenue streams lies with the board of directors. This may sound highly theoretical and formalistic, but that's not how the directors see it. Shareholders don't have the right to appropriate for themselves the assets, revenue, guarantees or products and services of the company without the explicit, formal approval of the board of directors. And if the board does intend to give such approval, it must ensure equal treatment for all shareholders. Moreover, not only the improper withdrawal of resources from the company but also any injection of resources into the enterprise comes under the supervision of the board of directors. A shareholder may not transfer any assets to the company without receiving the correct price in return. Once again, this is part of the duties of the directors, often with the assistance, as laid down in the relevant legislation, of external experts.

Directors also have a duty to provide shareholders with timely and accurate information. If this seems a blindingly obvious statement, actually fulfilling this obligation is harder than it may appear. For instance, a dividend payment has been announced and suddenly the board discovers that the company needs to raise extra funds. The directors have a duty to inform the shareholders as quickly as possible, but then the share price will probably fall and it will become even harder to stick to the company's strategic plan. Another example: the company announces the launch of a promising new product, but then it transpires that the product launch isn't working out. An announcement to this effect has of course to be made but that causes the new product to sink without trace. In such cases, directors are often torn between their duty to inform shareholders and their duty to the company, which deserves a chance to do the best thing for its future. I'll come back to this point later, when I discuss company press releases.

The situation is of course not the same for a non-listed firm or private limited liability company. At this kind of company, the directors can discuss matters with the shareholders and explain why the firm has become caught up in unfavourable circumstances and what exactly is going on, without the competition listening in.

NOT-FOR-PROFIT ORGANISATIONS

Not-for-profit organisations, i.e. enterprises, which – as we saw in the Introduction – are designated under Belgian law as 'associations' (including such entities as hospitals, cultural centres, educational establishments, NGOs, etc.), have rather special characteristics as regards the workings of the board of directors. They are of course entitled to run commercial activities, but any profits they make remain within the organisation and since they don't distribute profits and can't be sold or transferred to realise surplus value, they actually have no shareholders. All these organisations hold annual meetings (though without any shareholders) and are governed by a board of directors, but it goes without saying that the relationship between these two representative assemblies is not the same as in a listed, non-listed or private limited liability company. In fact, it's often the same members who attend the annual meeting and sit on the board of non-profit organisations. This means that the representatives attending the annual meeting cannot play the same role as shareholders of a for-profit limited liability company.

There isn't necessarily always this huge overlap between the annual meeting and the board of directors. If the organisation has a lot of members, they should all attend, or be represented at, the annual general meeting. But this is another example of how the context in which the board operates will condition its duties and way of working. The AGM of a non-profit organisation appoints the directors, grants them discharge for the work they've done, approves the accounts and agrees on the strategic direction the organisation should take. However, given the considerable overlap, we cannot really say that in such cases the AGM is exercising genuine supervision over the directors, even when all the members of the organisation attend the meeting.

At a not-for-profit organisation, the real supervision is usually carried out by the bodies that sponsor or subsidise the organisation. Most non-profits couldn't survive if they weren't able to rely on sponsorship or subsidies for a percentage of their budget. Even if they bring in extra income from commercial activities or members' contributions, these will not usually suffice to cover their running costs. This is why the directors are more accountable to sponsors and subsidy providers: they are the ones who will be looking to ensure that the organisation's mission and strategy are being carried out within the agreed budget. So it's clear that the board of a non-profit organisation, even one that has commercial activities, will be working under different constraints than the board of a for-profit firm. Obviously, the authorities who subsidise such organisations like to have a say in who sits on the board and who is appointed to chair it. This is often the only way to monitor the organisation's use of resources. It is of course clear that responsibility for rendering a full and transparent account of the use of all subsidies, sponsors' funds and members' contributions lies with the board of directors. Boards which use such funds for purposes other than the agreed goals will tend to damage the organisation's reputation and eventually jeopardise its future existence. Financial transparency requirements – regarding income, expenses, compensation, debts incurred and results achieved – which are incumbent on a for-profit company also apply to a non-profit organisation. This doesn't always happen, of course. In Belgium, there was the notorious case of Samusocial, a Brussels-based charity organisation whose directors were discovered in 2017 not to have acted with due care. This again illustrates how important it is to have a board of directors that works properly.

THE BALANCE OF POWER BETWEEN SHAREHOLDERS

Does the company have just one shareholder, several or many? This will have an enormous bearing on the duties of its board. The way the company stock is distributed between the various shareholders will also make a big difference. We can usefully differentiate between four basic situations: a highly fragmented shareholder structure; one dominant shareholder with broad fragmentation among the others; several blocks of shareholders, with perhaps one or more blocks assuming leadership (maybe in the form of a shareholder syndicate); and a company with one sole shareholder.

A fragmented shareholder structure

We mostly find instances of a highly fragmented shareholder structure at listed companies. Such companies are predominantly found in the United States and the UK. The phenomenon of fragmented shareholdership is much less common in European and Asian countries. There are however some examples in Belgium, such as Ageas. Fragmented shareholdership arose in the USA in the 1920s and 30s. This approach to financing companies was given the name 'managerial capitalism',[6] denoting the idea that when shareholdings become very small, the shareholders tend to lose power to the company managers or directors. This power shift was first described by Berle and Means in their world-renowned book *The Modern Corporation*

---

6 Alfred D. Chandler Jr. & Herman Daems (eds.) – *The Rise of Managerial Capitalism.* Harvard University Press, 1976.

and Private Property.[7] They reported that power was shifting mainly to management in such cases and they didn't see the board as an effective counterweight. Their book caused quite a stir worldwide and led to a wave of publications on the subject of company management and governance. It even led to a change in economic theory, because theoreticians came to the conclusion that managers – unlike shareholders – were likely to be more turnover-driven than profit-driven.

In a way, the corporate governance movement that arose in the UK and the USA in the 1970s and 80s was in response to managerial capitalism. When you have a fragmented shareholder structure, shareholders retain hardly any power over the management. As a consequence, managers are less interested in profit. They tend to make sizeable acquisitions which don't increase the profits or raise the value of the company but do boost management prestige. They spend money on things that are nice for the management – high salaries, comfortable offices, private aircraft, and so on – but bring no added value to the company. So the proponents of corporate governance argued that the board should keep an eye out for – and put a stop to – such extravagance. Two Harvard economists expressed this notion in very crisp terms: "*Corporate governance must prevent managers from stealing from the company.*"[8] Prior to that, the view that the directors were actually agents of the highly fragmented shareholders, who were no longer in a position to exercise effective supervision over the company, had gained ground. Thus the idea took hold that corporate governance was in fact one application of the 'agency' theory.

Last but not least, there arose in financial circles the expression 'shareholder value'. This notion was intended to help board members and managers to take decisions that would create value for the shareholders. There are a number of technical formulae designed to define and measure shareholder value. To put it briefly, the creation

<hr />

7 Transaction Publishers, 1932.

8 Andreii Schleifer and Robert W. Vishny – *A survey of Corporate Governance,* Journal of Finance, 1997 – Vol. 59 pp. 737-783

of shareholder value comes down to ensuring that the value of the company shares rises above the level of the money originally put in, appropriately corrected for the value of time. Both these notions – a) that the directors are agents of the shareholders and b) shareholder value as a touchstone for the board's performance – are still seen as valid in the English-speaking world. This is, as I will demonstrate later, a less accurate view of things as far as European countries are concerned. The reasons are obvious. European companies are not faced to the same extent with a fragmented shareholder structure and consequently undergo stricter supervision by their shareholders. Moreover, focus on shareholder value is diminishing as companies increasingly understand that they need to take account of the interests of others who are affected by their actions. Thus arose the idea of shared value – the value that's created for all those involved with or affected by the company.[9]

Boards that have to work with a fragmented shareholder structure must consequently ensure that the management doesn't let the shareholders down and that the strategies drawn up by management do actually create shareholder value. They should focus more closely than other boards on movements in the share price, because these will give an important clue as to what shareholders think of the directors and the management. Large sell-offs and a falling share price may be indications that the shareholders are dissatisfied. When a company has a more concentrated shareholder structure, which we'll be looking at in a moment, stock price movements play a lesser role in signalling to the board what shareholders really want, because directors can talk directly with shareholders and find out what they want. Obviously, with a fragmented shareholder structure, the board must also make sure that it provides full, accurate and timely information to shareholders, otherwise the share price will not correctly reflect the plans

9   Michael E. Porter & Mark R. Kramer – *Creating Shared Value: Redefining Capitalism and the role of the Corporation in Society*, Harvard Business Review, January 2011.

and policies being pursued by management. If directors fail to provide full, accurate information in a timely fashion, not only will they be manifestly misleading the shareholders but management won't get to know what the shareholders really think of their policies and the results achieved.

To help ensure that shareholders can rely on directors who are capable of forming an assessment independently of management, the corporate governance movement came up with the concepts of the non-executive director and independent director. The term non-executive director should be perfectly clear. It means a director who doesn't actively implement any decisions him/herself within the company. The expectation is that someone who isn't involved in executing decisions, policies and strategies will be able to show greater objectivity in assessing those decisions, policies and strategies. It's harder to give a precise definition of an independent director, as the criteria for 'independence' are not entirely clear. In some cases, a highly detailed description will be provided, such as the percentage of the company equity that such a director may hold, or the number of board seats that s/he may hold simultaneously. Others argue that it's important to have the right personal qualities – basically an independent mindset – so as to be able to maintain his/her own view of events, without being overly influenced by the management.

No-one seriously disputes any longer that having good independent and non-executive directors on the board helps to ensure that it functions properly. However, the question of who possesses the right characteristics to be a good independent director will always remain a matter for debate. In fact, I'm becoming increasingly convinced that, like so many other things regarding the board of directors, the performance of an independent director also depends on the context in which s/he has to work. If s/he finds him/herself sitting on the board of a company with a fragmented shareholder structure, the required characteristics will not be the same as if s/he has to deal with a dominant shareholder. An independent director will not always find it easy to go up against a 'reference shareholder' who, at the end of the day, will have to decide whether or not to renew his/her mandate. It's also sometimes an open question as to whether non-executive and independent directors who are obliged to act as agents of the shareholders will have the right knowledge and motivation. I'll come back later to the complex issue of directors' emoluments.

A concentrated shareholder structure or a reference shareholder

In most Belgian companies and very many firms all over continental Europe, Russia and Asia, you'll find a controlling shareholder alongside a number of minority shareholders who individually don't have the power to decide the direction in which the company should go. The holder of this controlling stake is generally known as the 'reference shareholder'. To put it simply, this is the shareholder whom the board and the management have to pay most attention to, as s/he will be able to wield power at the AGM.

Sometimes you will hear it said that, in order to wield power, a reference shareholder needs to hold at least 50% of the company's issued equity. In theory that's correct and this view usually holds true in times of serious crisis at the firm. In normal times however, if we're talking about approving the accounts, granting discharge to the directors or deciding on the appointment of directors or managers, this is not the case. If you want to measure the power of a reference shareholder, you need to calculate things in a different way. I always start out from the percentage of shares that will actually be directly voted or represented by proxy at the AGM or EGM. That is rarely 100%. At the companies in which I've been involved, I think probably on average 60% of the equity was represented at AGMs. In such cases, a reference shareholder needs to hold only 30% of the issued shares in order to exercise control at the meeting and decide on all the resolutions tabled, except where the statutes stipulate a specific 'qualified' majority, such as for instance 75%. Most reference

> Sometimes you can exercise control over a company with just 30% of the equity.

shareholders therefore prefer to hold a larger stake in the company so that they can be sure of obtaining the decisions they want on all resolutions tabled at the meeting.

Now that 'loyalty voting rights' may be on the way in some European countries (for instance a double vote for each share held for a period of two years) these calculations are likely to change and smaller stakes will suffice to achieve a 'reference shareholder' position. The proponents of double voting rights in Belgium believe that this will make it harder for foreign parties to take over Belgian companies. This is a rather odd point of view, because very few hostile takeovers have occurred in Belgium. Most takeovers by foreign companies have gone through with the full approval of the reference shareholder. With double voting rights it's therefore likely to be easier, not harder, to carry through such acquisitions. Moreover, double voting rights will enable a large shareholder to control the company with less capital, without having to pay out any compensation. I'm not convinced that this will be a positive development.

When a firm has a concentrated shareholder structure and a reference shareholder, that will create an entirely different situation for the board of directors. There'll be several directors sitting on the board who represent the reference shareholder, alongside a number of independent directors, whose role should be to defend the interests of the smaller shareholders. So there you have a board where different interests are present but which should nevertheless strive to ensure that the interests of the company are paramount.

Clearly the board of directors at a company with a reference shareholder must first and foremost try to ensure that the various shareholders receive equal treatment. This is quite different from the situation at a firm with a fragmented shareholder structure, where the directors must endeavour to maintain a balance of power between management and shareholders and see to it that the latter's interests are not pushed aside by the former. As I mentioned earlier, it's an important part of a director's duties at a company with a fragmented shareholder structure to solve the notorious 'agency problem'. Where there's a reference shareholder however, the board needs to ensure that this large shareholder doesn't take unfair advantage of the weak position of the minority shareholders. There are a lot of areas of decision-making where dangers may be lurking, such as transfers of assets between two companies that are both in the hands of one and the same reference shareholder, dividend policy, the buying out of minority interests at non-market prices, etc., or the other way round: when assets belonging to the reference shareholder are bought by the company at too high a price, or when policies drawn up and carried out are in the interest of the group of companies to which the reference shareholder belongs but not in the interest of the shareholders of this individual company. This can happen, for instance, when the reference shareholder doesn't support proposals for international expansion because this dominant shareholder has other holdings abroad and doesn't want to see those other companies facing any new competition.

The example above provides a striking illustration of how the interests of a company, and its minority shareholders, can differ from those of the majority shareholder. This may require a balancing act from the directors, whose duty will thus differ from what's expected of them in a fragmented shareholder structure. Similar examples can arise when it comes to the development of new technology and new products, where the reference shareholder would prefer – on efficiency grounds – to see the development work transferred to a specialised plant. This makes sense from the majority shareholder's point of view, because the technological development can then be optimised across the group as a whole. It might well however be highly disadvantageous for the minority shareholders of the company, who will just have to accept that its competitiveness will diminish and they'll then become dependent on what the reference shareholder does at the other site.

So it's quite clear that the duties of directors working with a fragmented shareholder structure are different from a situation where there's a dominant shareholder at the company. Independent directors will nevertheless be needed in both types of structure in order to ensure that the company is run in a balanced way. However, appointing genuinely independent directors in the second case is going to pose a problem because, as we described above, the dominant shareholder will usually command a majority, or near majority, of votes at the AGM and will therefore be in a position to have the independent directors that s/he wants appointed and will have a decisive say in their subsequent re-appointment. So we have here a strange situation. Directors who are supposed to defend the interests of minority shareholders are basically appointed and re-appointed by the majority shareholder. To my personal knowledge, this way of doing things has never led to outright abuse – i.e. that directors who exercise critical judgement are never re-appointed – but it's nonetheless an uncomfortable situation for the directors to be in and it requires the dominant shareholder to understand exactly what the role of an independent director actually is in such cases.

For instance, Belgian company law provides for directors to be removed from office at any time, without the need to give reasons for the dismissal (what is known as the *ad nutum* principle) and in principle also forbids the granting of any dismissal compensation or severance payments. This is remarkable because these two principles render directors – and this is especially true of so-called independent directors – entirely dependent on the open-mindedness of a dominant shareholder. As described above, at critical moments directors need to find the right balance between the interests of the reference shareholder and those of the minority shareholders. So it's definitely odd that in Belgium they can be dismissed on the spot and forced to depart without any compensation. This basically means that directors can either stand up for what they believe and risk suffering adverse consequences or fall in line with the reference shareholder. Quite a difference from judges and civil servants who can rely on lifelong appointments intended to safeguard their independence! So far, independent directors haven't

So-called 'independent' directors are in fact totally dependent on the open-mindedness of the reference shareholder.

needed such special protection. Fortunately, the legislators' thinking is evolving somewhat and severance compensation can now be obtained under certain circumstances. However, Belgian law doesn't yet provide real protection for independent company directors.

Another problem that may arise with dominant shareholders is that they will tend to dig more deeply into the organisation. They'll keep a sharp eye on the company's financial department and they may take a close interest in other departments as well. This means that the board of directors must be aware that a dominant shareholder will be well informed. Of course, this is less important when the company is listed on the stock exchange, because then the reference shareholder will in any case have foreknowledge of the expected results but will at the very least be expected not to use – or allow relatives to use – this inside information to actively engage in trading in the shares of the company.

Just to be absolutely clear, I should point out here that if the dominant shareholder in a company does not hold any other related stakes and is not actually a group of companies with various subsidiaries, the problems outlined above will be less acute or may not arise at all.

Multiple shareholder blocks

In a company, we sometimes also find several blocks of shareholders. Examples of this are a family firm where perhaps four branches of the family each holds 25% of the equity, or a technology company where perhaps each of five venture capital funds has a significant packet of shares and the management or founding entrepreneurs still retain sizeable stakes.

It will come as no surprise when I say that in such circumstances the board of directors will once again differ in terms of its composition, duties and way of working. First, a word about the composition. When a company's shareholder structure is made up of a number of blocks of shareholders, each block will be able to nominate and secure the election of several directors, who will be complemented by a few independent directors. The board then becomes a forum for the various shareholder interests and usually, in such cases, there will be a preference for an independent chairperson who doesn't belong to any of the blocks. The role of the independent directors is then to ensure that friction between the various blocks and the different directors remains manageable.

If the blocks consist mainly of venture capital funds or professional investors, the board's main task will be to prepare the company for a stock market flotation or sale to another company. We often see this pattern in the life sciences or biotech sector. An enterprise is founded by one or more research scientists, who recruit a professional CEO to run the business and go in search of professional investors from the venture capital world. Those investors will of course only be able to make a return on their investment if some years later they're able to arrange an Initial Public Offering (IPO) or a takeover by another firm. Directors at this sort of startup and growth company will usually be specialists in a particular aspect of the biotech sector or else adept at selling off businesses or floating companies on the stock market. In this case, the board will also be closely involved in the day-to-day running of the enterprise. I'm not suggesting that the directors will be incorrigible busybodies and meddlers but a startup will probably not have the specialists available to do all the management jobs, which will leave room for directors to lend a hand now and again in the running of the company.

If the block-type shareholder structure is made up of a number of families or different branches of a single family, there ought to be several independents sitting on the board of directors who can help to make the board's decision-making more objective.

When the shareholdership is made up of a number of families, it's not unusual to find members of those families working inside the organisation or in the management team. This means once again that the independent directors will be faced with fellow directors who are very familiar with all the ins and outs of the company business. This may be an entirely positive thing, but it can also mean that the independents have much less information than their fellow directors from the family groupings.

We do not only find shareholder blocks in cases where various family interests or a number of specialised risk capital or venture capital funds have equity stakes. Such blocks can also be the result of several companies or investors deciding to pool their money, knowledge and skills to set up a new venture. The boards of joint ventures, for instance, are usually composed of representatives of the founding entities. Sometimes independent directors are also appointed but they won't be there to represent the interests of one group of shareholders. They'll be there due to their technological or market knowledge or their personal network, and also to help keep the peace between the various joint venture partners.

Sole shareholder

Sometimes a company will be in the hands of a single shareholder. This may be literally the case, but it can also happen that several shareholders tend to engage in mutual consultation to the extent that for all practical purposes they speak with one voice. Again, this might be a family situation, where several of the children hold shares and a parent acting on their behalf takes all necessary decisions. Generally, when there's only one shareholder, s/he will be closely involved in the management of the company and will let everyone know who's really in charge. There's a high probability that s/he actually set up the business and knows the firm inside out.

Sole shareholder situations are found not only in family companies. This approach is also frequently used in the corporate world to run a group of companies. So what is the role of a board of directors within corporate structures with basically one single shareholder? Or more precisely: what is the role of independent directors in this type of framework? Is it useful to have independent directors here at all? To answer these questions, we should perhaps reiterate here that directors are elected at the AGM. At sole-shareholder firms, 100% of the voting shares are by definition in the hands of one shareholder. Consequently, an independent director will depend on this one person or entity for his/her appointment and subsequent re-appointment and will certainly not have the same role as independent directors at companies with a fragmented shareholder structure, a reference shareholder or several shareholder blocks. Given that the shareholder is so closely involved in the running of the company, the agency problem will hardly arise at all and there'll also be no need to seek a balance between the interests of majority and minority shareholders, or of a number of shareholders of equal weight in the firm.

Nevertheless, we increasingly find independent shareholders on the boards of sole-shareholder companies. One of the reasons is that sole shareholders have come to realise that they might sometimes need input from an external expert in order to form an opinion on how the business is going and the investment that will be required. This is no easy task. What if the shareholder is in favour of a particular idea and the independent director against? Conflict might arise between shareholder and director and it's not hard to foresee that the director might well get short shrift when his/her mandate comes up for renewal! I know from experience however, that independent directors can be of great value in this sort of company because of the outside perspective they can bring. But they do need to be diplomatic in so doing. On the other hand, we might expect that a sole shareholder who brings an independent director into the enterprise will be willing to take a sufficiently open-minded attitude. If the shareholder decides to bring a director in, then s/he should at least be given a chance to do her job properly. And that job is precisely to help the company make the best possible decisions by contributing knowledge and opinions from outside the firm. The independent director must therefore be well-qualified and credible; otherwise, his/her contribution will be no greater than a puppet in a Punch-and-Judy show.

The shareholder structure of a company will thus be determined on the one hand by the number of shareholders involved and the balance of power between them. On the other hand, the type of shareholder invested in the company will also have an impact on the shareholder structure and on the tasks that fall to the board of directors. I'll discuss this in the next few paragraphs.

SHAREHOLDER TYPES

We could almost say that there are as many types of shareholders as there are shareholders! Every shareholder has his/her own special characteristics, which differentiate him/her from other shareholders. However, I think it will be useful to sketch out a number of shareholder types, as each type will have a different kind of impact on the duties and working of the board of directors of a limited company or not-for-profit organisation.

> There are perhaps as many types of shareholders as there are shareholders.

It makes sense to differentiate between individual investors, investment funds, investment companies, venture capital specialists, private equity investors, groups of companies or other firms, family shareholders, the state and social enterprises or civil society groupings.

Individual investors

Investors are people who buy a packet of shares in a company in the hope that the equity will increase in value or that they'll obtain a nice annual dividend on their holding. These shareholders want the board of directors to ensure that they don't lose their capital or see the value of their stake diminish and that they don't find their interests pushed aside by management or a dominant shareholder. They see the board as monitors of management. They know about potential agency problems – when management tries to cheat the shareholders – and they count on the company directors to prevent that happening.

Some investors hold a relatively small stake in a listed company over many years and show up regularly at the AGM. They often provide a certain degree of stability in the shareholder structure, although this will be only small-scale stability and if a big storm starts to blow among the shareholders, they will not be in a position to play a dominant role. The drawback with this type of shareholder is that they don't do much to improve liquidity in the company shares. Then there's another kind of investor who is constantly buying and selling shares. Some of the more active ones become day traders, who hold any given company's shares for a very short time. What does this mean for directors? Short-term investors are unlikely to attend the AGM or vote for the (re)appointment of directors. Nevertheless, the board needs to take them into account. They help to determine the share price and will tend to react fast to any breaking news about the firm. This is one reason why the board must take great care to ensure that the company's financial communication is accurate and clear.

Investment funds

Investment funds are now taking on an ever-greater importance for companies. Their analysts will track the company on a daily basis, question the management and use models to try to forecast the financial results. Some, though not all, investment funds will speak up at the AGM and express their views about the company policies, the management and the board. Moreover, investment funds are now increasingly international in their operations, which enables and encourages them to compare companies' strategies and results on an international basis. They're not impressed by a parochial approach and want to see highly professional company policies and extremely professional governance.

> Investment funds want to see extremely professional governance rather than a parochial approach.

Nowadays, ever more investment funds follow a portfolio strategy. Sometimes this will be based on an index strategy. They will then take a stake in a given company on the basis of the parameters of the portfolio model. The model will take account of risk and return, plus also a number of factors likely to determine the evolution of the share price. This kind of approach leaves very little room for interaction with the board of directors. Everything will be decided on the basis of hard figures and risk assessments, with calculations of covariance with other equities and 'beta' volatility measurements in relation to other traded securities. The board is expected to ensure that the company's performance and results are predictable and that the forecast results are actually achieved. If forecast plans and results are not achieved, the directors can expect merciless punishment from the investment fund managers.

There's one class of funds which board members and managers can find particularly annoying. These are known as 'activist' funds. Their basic strategy is to obtain seats on the boards of listed companies or at least to force changes in company policy, with the aim of driving up the share price. They usually buy up sufficiently large stakes in order to have their voices heard and take other shareholders along with them in their opposition to current policies and management. As a first step they often 'short' the stock, i.e. they sell shares they don't actually hold in the expectation of buying them back at a lower price when they've successfully driven the price down. They don't always succeed in their aims. Moreover, you can sometimes persuade activists to pack up and go by offering them inducements. One might be tempted to describe such activists as no better than a band of robbers but that would actually be too negative a view of things because activist funds can also help to get things moving at a company. In fact, their aim is not always to make money from the situation; sometimes their intention is to force the company to adopt more environmentally-friendly, socially responsible or humanitarian behaviour. As far as the directors are concerned, this means they'll need to assess precisely what the real intentions of a given activist fund are and should carefully consider any suggestions that might make a real difference. Here again, though, they'll need to weigh up the pros and cons because not all shareholders will want to go along with the proposals made by activist funds. Following the proposals of one group of shareholders can lead to problems with other shareholder groups that wish to pursue other interests.

In recent years it's also become clear that the movement for more responsible and sustainable corporate behaviour is not only being driven by activist funds. Ever more investment funds and pension funds have also drawn up a code of conduct and encourage companies to abide by its principles. Examples range from funds that manage money on behalf of universities to some very large pension funds in California, Canada, Scotland and Norway. They don't want companies to continue investing in such areas as tobacco products or pollutant mining activities. They're often supported in this policy by the banks that are called upon to provide lending to those companies. What this means for the boards of those companies is that they'll either have to take account of what the funds want or else go and look for other shareholders.

Investment funds are likely to take on greater importance for larger stock exchange-listed firms and smaller listed companies that wish to build a more international shareholdership. The increasing weight of investment funds is also changing the character of shareholder structures. There's more emphasis on results and also on the short term. In such cases, there no longer exists any real emotional connection between the company and its shareholders. Shareholders who are confronted with unsatisfactory company results have three options: they can speak up and express their dissatisfaction – what the corporate governance literature often calls the 'voice option'; they can remain loyal to the company in the belief or hope that the good times will eventually return – the 'loyalty option'; or they sell off their stake in the firm – the 'exit option'. At companies in which investment funds have taken stakes, the exit option is going to become more prevalent, and consequently, the directors will need to take increasing account of share price movements as a signal of what their shareholders want.

Do activist funds act like a band of robbers? In fact, they often manage to get things moving at a company.

Investment companies

Belgian investment companies, such as GBL, Sofina and Ackermans&
VanHaaren, build portfolios of holdings in mostly non-listed companies. They make an effort to maintain a diverse portfolio so as to
spread the investment risk, but they certainly don't strive to construct
an optimally diversified portfolio based on a meticulously calculated
risk-return model. The approach taken by investment companies is to
try to influence the board, the management, the strategy, the financing
and the results of companies in which they hold stakes. Sometimes
they will be the reference shareholder, in other cases they'll hold a
significant minority stake and their holding will of course be reflected
in the composition, duties and workings of the board of directors.

An investment company will not usually attempt to get the various
companies in its portfolio working together; each of them will be
viewed independently. This doesn't of course rule out the possibility
that there'll be some degree of coordination at the financial level
and also as regards a number of support services, but this will not
be central to what the investment company is trying to achieve. It
will endeavour first and foremost to provide careful support for the
running of the companies in the portfolio in order to achieve the best
possible results and boost their value to the maximum. Moreover,
investment companies are not known for making fast exits from
companies. Very often, they prove to be long-term shareholders.

The basic task of the board of directors of a company which forms
part of the portfolio of an investment company or investment fund
is to enable the business to deliver the best possible performance
and, to this end, to provide the necessary support at the strategic and
operational levels. The board will closely monitor management and
quickly ascertain whether the management is in a position to attain
the targets set.

An investment company will nearly always obtain direct representation on the board of directors, even if it has only a minority holding,
and whenever an investment company is the reference shareholder

in the firm, it will insist on appointing the board chair. Sometimes independent directors will be given seats on the board. This may happen because the law so requires, as is the case with a portfolio company that's also listed on the stock exchange, or because the investment company wants to bring a number of experts into the business, or because independent directors are needed to ensure objective decision-making that takes account of the interests of the various shareholders involved. The directors will basically need to keep a close eye on the strategy, the capital investments under consideration with a view to achieving the strategy, the attainment of the business plans and the performance of the management.

Venture capitalists and private equity investors

Risk capital specialists come in three kinds: private equity firms, buyout groups, and venture capitalists. They're usually organised in the form of funds, such as the Belgium-based buyout fund Waterland and US-headquartered CVC, or private equity funds and venture capital funds such as Capricorn and Gemma Frisius. Others function as investment companies. The chief goal of these three types of risk capital providers is to achieve a sizeable leap in value as rapidly as possible for companies which they helped to set up or in which they hold a stake. As a minimum they'll be looking to double their money when they sell the stake or, as the sector jargon puts it: to achieve an exit multiple[10] of at least 2.

Most risk capital firms are still striving for a return of around 25% on the cash they invested in the company, although due to the current long period of low interest rates returns are often now much lower. Nevertheless, high returns are still the norm, mainly because the risks inherent in this sort of investment are extremely high. Currently, a

---

10 The *exit multiple* is the relationship between the sum initially invested in the company and the amount obtained when the company is sold.

high internal rate of return (IRR) is only attainable if the exit multiple is very high and the investment is of a relatively short duration. In this area, the financial maths is inescapable. If you're looking for a high IRR, you'll need to achieve a high exit multiple and not leave your cash in the business too long either. The one approach precludes the other. The fact that most risk capital funds aim not to remain a shareholder in any company for too long – usually somewhere between seven and ten years – also of course has consequences for the way the board works and the role of the directors. The investment horizon for a risk capital fund is determined by the fact that these are often closed-end funds. This means that it collects money from investors who want to liquidate their investment within a certain time span. This funding technique forces most risk capital funds to take shareholdings whose value is likely to rise sharply in the mid-term.

So how can the value of a company be made to rise rapidly? There are basically three possibilities:

1 Management can opt for a strategy of fast revenue growth, counting on economies of scale, or else the company succeeds in turning its burgeoning market share into higher margins, causing a rise in the annual cash flow and consequently in the value of the company. As part of this strategic path, you can also pursue an active corporate acquisition strategy – taking over competitors or companies that will extend your value chain. Venture capitalists talk here about a 'buy and build strategy'.

2 Management can decide to undertake a financial restructuring of the company. This entails sharply pushing up the company's debt ratio and then subsequently using the cash flows to pay off the debt. At first, the share value will be low, due to the high indebtedness, but once the debt has been reduced, the value of the equity will rise. Other variations on this theme are possible, such as executing a temporary capital reduction, which will be financed by taking on new debt.

3 The third way to boost the value of a company is to split up the business into its component parts. Those components will often be worth more independently than when fused together. If the

components can be sold off at a good price, the total value of the original investment will rise.

It will be obvious to the reader that the board of an enterprise that's in the hands of a number of venture capitalists will look very different from a standard governing body. The directors sitting round the table usually come from risk capital funds. Now and then they'll call upon so-called 'independent' directors who aren't directly involved with one of the funds represented, but then they'll need to bring in top-quality specialists in those markets or technologies with which the company works, or experts with experience of carrying out thorough company transformations. A financial expert might also be useful. You sometimes also find observers sitting on this kind of board. In actual fact these people are not really directors, and although they attend board meetings, they have no vote. This can occur when there are rather a lot of venture capital firms involved and there's a need to keep the board to a reasonable size.

The duty of the directors of a venture capital-owned company is clear. They must take steps to ensure that the value of the company rises in as short a time as possible and that it becomes an attractive proposition for acquisition by another firm or for an initial public offering (IPO) on the stock market. To ensure that the directors and management are properly aligned with the venture capitalists, holders of these top posts

> The duty of the directors of venture capital-owned companies is clear: to prepare the company for a takeover or IPO.

often receive variable compensation packages, a phenomenon that we find much less often with other kinds of boards. The directors' duties mainly consist of monitoring the business plan drawn up by executive management in discussion with the venture capitalists. Any deviation from the plan will bring an immediate reaction from the directors and shareholders because everyone understands that this may jeopardise the company's debt financing programme. There'll also of course be a lot of discussion about strategy, particularly if we're talking about a startup, where a less precise business plan may be drawn up. These directors are also fully aware that they will only be involved with the company for a relatively short period.

Groups of companies

Groups work in a different way. For a group of companies, it's all about ensuring that synergies exist between the companies in which the group holds stakes and that those synergies are actually realised. There may be synergies in all kinds of areas: a coordinated strategy for all group companies; joint R&D; common suppliers; choice of customers and the sharing of markets or market segments across the various group companies; joint distribution channels; and the use of common brand names. Synergies may also be connected with the norms and standards of the group, human resources policy and compensation policy. The group will also be involved in the management recruitment policy of the companies within the group.

It's not easy for the board of directors of one of the group companies – and there certainly will have to be a board for legal reasons because the individual companies within the group are generally set up as legally separate entities – to work under this kind of group structure. Group central management will be closely involved in deciding the composition of the board and will also take steps to ensure that several people from the group are appointed directors at the subsidiary company. However, it's more than likely that there'll be some independent directors as well, sometimes because there'll also be local minority shareholders but also because the group will want to ensure that the subsidiary engages with the local community. This point is of great importance if the subsidiary also has to serve the local market.

The difficulty for the board in such cases is to find the right balance between what needs to be done in order to carry out group strategy and realise the synergies, the desire to grant the subsidiary – which is a legally independent entity – a credible degree of autonomy without damaging the interests of the group, and not losing sight of the fact that board members remain legally responsible for what happens at and around the company. On the one hand, the search for balance in this kind of board can lead to total passivity, where it's just taken for granted that the most important decisions are taken elsewhere and all the directors have to do is rubber-stamp them. Alternatively, it can lead to battles between the group and its individual subsidiaries. Neither of these situations is desirable and both must be avoided at all costs. The problem can be solved by bringing people on to the board who enjoy credibility in the group structure because of their skills or reputation, but then there must also be a clear understanding at central group level that the board of directors at a subsidiary company does have a role of its own to play, given the legal independence of the subsidiary and the formal responsibility incumbent on the directors.

The whole governance question has become much more complex over the last 20 years due to changes in group structures. Up to about 30 years ago, groups of companies were mainly organised along national lines and this national organisation was usually in line with the legal framework. In those days, the Belgian subsidiary of a group used to be a fully-fledged organisational unit that dovetailed perfectly with the legal unit, which made things a lot simpler for the board. Now groups are organised by business line, which means that the organisational structure of the group seldom corresponds with the legal structure. Thus it can happen that a Belgium-based subsidiary isn't in charge of managing all its activities. This is quite difficult for the board, since part of the activities that will determine the company's results doesn't fall under the responsibility of those directors. This can of course all be arranged perfectly well within the group, provided that there's effective cooperation and transparent reporting, but it will require mutual trust to be built up.

Family shareholders

Family shareholders pose problems of a different kind for the board of directors. In my experience, families always seem to have a double objective: maintaining pride in the family legacy, alongside the desire to preserve and increase the family fortune. As far as the directors are concerned, this means that some options – such as selling off the business or relocating the operations – are more or less a no-go area.

One thorny problem sometimes arises when a number of different branches of a family hold stakes in the firm and the business needs to be recapitalised. In such cases, it can happen that not all the branches of the family think in the same way about injecting fresh capital or don't possess the same capacity to supply the new capital. This confronts the directors with a delicate task that will require careful consideration and creative solutions. It might be possible to raise the new capital from third parties – but then the family would have to share some of their decision-making power – or by taking out a loan, which will increase the company's exposure to risk.

Another tricky problem can arise if the company has to be restructured. Family groupings may differ over how thoroughgoing the remediation needs to be, how many employees will be made redundant and who is responsible for the downturn in affairs. This last question is definitely problematic if not all branches of the family have been involved in running the company.

The state as shareholder

Federal and regional government, provincial or local authorities, plus also all kinds of public sector institutions may hold stakes in companies and organisations. They may do so for a wide variety of reasons – sometimes to ensure that a particular service is provided to the population, sometimes so as to keep control over certain activities, sometimes in order to guarantee financing, or provide support. This latter reason has certainly been the case with banks in Belgium, although at the back of some politicians' minds there was probably also the desire to (re)assert control over parts of the banking sector.

In fact, we find the state and public sector organisations taking a hand in quite a number of economic sectors, from waste collection and treatment to anti-poverty initiatives, telecommunications and even private equity. To run all these government and social initiatives, the authorities need quite a number of directors sitting on dozens of boards. In fact, I wouldn't be at all surprised if there were more people acting as directors in the public sector on behalf of the government than there are board members in the private sector.

The boards of many state-run or public sector establishments are often somewhat torn between the authorities and the public sector on the one hand and the organisation for which they're supposed to be responsible on the other. In fact, in Belgium, for instance, the state and public authorities will not hesitate to intervene directly and make public statements about what they think ought to be happening at the organisa-tion. Such shareholder conduct is very unusual at a private sector company, but the authorities often justify their approach with declarations like: 'As politicians, we have to step in because that's what the voters require of us.' This is perhaps under-standable, but why don't they explain to the voters that such direct interventions make it impossible to run the organisation properly? Why don't they ask the directors to make a statement? That seems more sensible to me and would enable the board of directors to fulfil its duties.

> The state is a shareholder that will not hesitate to have its say about the organisation.

One of the board's standard tasks is to monitor the use of the organisation's resources. Directors are assisted in this task by audi-tors. It would make more sense for the public authorities to follow the same principle rather than appointing special commissioners to do this very same job, as is the case in Belgium. If there's any suspicion of improper use of resources, it would be better to call the board to account, as is done at limited liability companies. That would keep the directors involved and give them the chance to do their jobs properly. Nowadays it appears that quite

> In Belgium, it appears that nowadays quite a number of government-appointed directors hold seats on governing bodies as a pure formality, without having any real job to do there.

a number of government-appointed directors in Belgium have seats on governing bodies as a pure formality, without having any real job to do there. The government ought to be working with the bodies that are supposed to be responsible for governance and supervision and not shoe-horning in new parallel bodies.

In a company or organisation where the state or the public sector holds a majority or a very significant stake, there will be several government-appointed representatives on the board. This is perfectly normal and we shouldn't see these directors as political appointees, provided that they possess the right expertise and bear in mind the purpose and interests of the company or organisation on whose board they're sitting. It's also perfectly reasonable that the composition of the board of such firms will change after the latest elections. The new government, which has won a majority for the new programme it proposes to carry out, might well see the need for a different board at some establishments. However, if the new directors are incompetent or unfamiliar with the organisation's goals and don't stand up for the purpose and interests of the company or organisation, then we can reasonably accuse the government of making political appointments and behaving in an arbitrary manner.

The Belgian state is also a shareholder, alongside others, in such stock exchange-listed corporations as Proximus, Belfius, Bpost, Gimv, and the European banking sector leader BNP Paribas. This places particular constraints on the government's action vis-à-vis the boards of those companies and the government-appointed directors who sit on them. The first thing that the government and the public sector ought to do is follow the corporate governance rules that have been laid down. Secondly, the government needs to realise that a majority at a company AGM isn't the same thing as a majority in Parliament. In Parliament, the government generally takes no notice of the minority, who are – after all – in opposition, not in office. However, it doesn't work quite like that in a limited liability company, because the minority shareholders always have the option of selling their stakes if they lose confidence in the government as reference shareholder.

Sometimes the government goes to the opposite extreme. Instead of taking a close interest in the company and trying to support the firm as a reference shareholder should, the government might decide to stay on the sidelines, abstaining on many decisions in the AGM for fear of having to render account of its actions in Parliament. In such cases, it would be better if the government were simply to withdraw from that company, because it will be creating absolutely no added value from a governance point of view. Moreover, selling off its holding would help to improve the state's overall debt ratio. If the government's sole reason for deciding to maintain the state's holding in the company is to protect it from a hostile takeover, it really ought to consider whether it could find another way, through legislation or regulation, to protect the firm in the event of a hostile takeover bid from abroad.

A government-appointed director in a state-owned company also needs to understand that s/he isn't sitting on the board as a representative of a particular political party. It may well be that his/her name was put forward by one party but his/her primary duty is to ensure that the company meets its targets in the most efficient manner. Anything else is a pure waste of talent and board time.

No shareholders

As mentioned above, charity organisations and non-profits have no shareholders, but we also find for-profit companies that have no real shareholders either. This happens for instance in the Netherlands, where entities known as *stichtingen* (foundations) hold stakes in companies but have no shareholders themselves. In such cases, the board of directors has no sounding-board. AGMs do take place, but these meetings usually echo what the board wishes to do and will not exercise meticulous supervision.

At first glance it might seem like a dream come true: being able to exercise governance over an organisation without having to take account of awkward shareholders! However, it's not quite as simple as that. For instance, what strategy should this type of company be pursuing? Should it be looking for growth, scaling up or going international? Where are you going to find extra risk capital? Or is all expansion going to be financed by taking on extra debt? And who bears the risk if things go wrong? Suppose the enterprise gets into difficulties due to a changing market or changes to the subsidy arrangements. Who will help to finance the necessary restructuring? These examples clearly demonstrate that, in order to be able to do their work properly, directors need shareholders as well as managers. The managers' job is to carry out the strategic plans; the function of shareholders is to provide financing. It's only through a combination of these two elements that the board of directors will be able to perform its duties.

> Governance without any shareholders: it might sound like a dream come true but it isn't.

Factor 2 Division of responsibilities

The shareholder structure is one of the factors, perhaps the most important one, that determine the context in which the board of directors has to work. As we saw in the preceding pages, the shareholder structure determines vital aspects of the composition, duties and workings of the governing body. A second factor is the division of powers and responsibilities between the AGM and the board. This factor can often lead to serious tensions. One example of this is the conflict that raged between late 2008 and early 2009 between the board of the former Fortis Group and the AGM. The shareholders – initially backed by the courts – disputed the board's right to sell a significant portion of the Fortis Group, namely Fortisbank, to the state, which would then sell the bank on to the BNP Paribas group. Subsequently, the board won the argument and obtained the support of a majority of the shareholders. However, before it did so, a noisy EGM took place that has now become part of corporate legend. This sort of major public conflict is very rare. Nevertheless, the issue of the division of powers and responsibilities is an important one, about which thick academic tomes have been written.[11]

The division of powers and responsibilities is laid down in the company statutes. This is a document with which every director needs to be fully familiar. Directors make proposals regarding the division of powers but the shareholders will have to approve them by a large majority. Nowadays it's more and more often the case that the directors set rules for conduct and ways of working at board level. Sometimes, however, rules of this kind are imposed on them. An example of this is a corporate governance statement. This is a positive development because this kind of declaration indicates that the directors are taking seriously the need for good governance at the company or organisation. However, they need to take care that such statements and statutes match up and are not mutually contradictory. If the statutes say nothing about what the directors must do or not do in the event of a takeover bid, and then the corporate governance statement published by the board contains a promise that shareholders will be consulted prior to any takeover going through, then shareholders might well get confused about what's really going to happen in such cases.

At family companies, the shareholders usually get more involved in fundamental decisions taken by the board of directors, or at least they expect to be thoroughly informed. This is why a lot of family businesses in Europe hold 'family council' sessions in addition to the AGMs. The purpose of this body is mostly not to take decisions but to keep the family properly informed about the company plans and results and what the policy is regarding the hiring of family members to do jobs at the company. It's perfectly understandable that the families wish to be fully informed and also to have their point of

11 For instance, Sofie Cools – *Bevoegdheidsverdeling tussen algemene vergadering en raad van bestuur in de NV [Division of Powers between the AGM and the Board of Directors in a Limited Liability Company]*. Roularta Media Group, 2015.

view heard when it comes to major capital investments. After all, these will have direct consequences for the dividend policy and/or – if new loans have to be taken out – for the company's overall risk position. It may be that the new investment will require a capital increase. In this case, the shareholders are directly affected: either they'll have to subscribe the new equity themselves or else allow an outsider to take a stake in the business, which will dilute the family's holding and control. Such decisions may radically alter the family's position in the company.

I mentioned earlier that whenever the state becomes involved in a company or organisation, either as shareholder or financier, the authorities may feel under strong pressure to intervene directly in the running of the enterprise without involving the governing body. The company statutes may well offer some protection as regards maintaining the existing division of powers but this isn't always a certainty.

At not-for-profit entities, the AGM frequently coincides with board sessions. In such cases, the general meeting becomes just a formality – confirming, or taking for a second time, the board's decisions. No wonder then that some directors see this process as a time-wasting exercise.

Factor 3 The composition of the board of directors

The third factor determining the context within which the board of directors performs its duties is the actual composition of the board. It's useful to take a three-dimensional view of this. One dimension is geared to the various categories of director sitting on the board, a second dimension has to do with the skills possessed by the directors and the third dimension is the gender balance. The number of people sitting on the board is also an important factor because it is of course easier to create a diversified board if there are a lot of seats on the governing body, but then that tends to raise other problems.

DIRECTOR CATEGORIES

Independent, executive... or not

When looking at the make-up of a board, we traditionally differentiate between independent, non-independent, executive and non-executive directors. It's obvious what you don't want on a board: all the directors performing the same function. If you only have executive directors – which is not uncommon at small family businesses where the board of directors tends to coalesce with management – in-depth critical analysis is often in short supply when decisions are being taken. By this I don't mean that there aren't enough experts on the board. It's precisely *because* they're all experts that the risk arises that the directors won't be able to think 'out of the box' and may lack the wisdom to take a new approach. If the only experience the directors have is of that company and its traditional markets, there won't be anyone on the board who is capable of asking searching questions about the strategic assumptions that have prevailed for years about technological evolution, distribution channels, production processes and customers. The need for deeper strategic debate and sharper critical analysis of the way the company is being run and the effectiveness of the management is an important reason why you should have non-executive directors on the board. Sometimes it's also said that it's harder to exercise supervision if all the directors have an executive role. This is not necessarily so, especially if we're talking about a family firm and family members are working in its executive management. However, the directors will still want to keep an eye on their colleagues to avoid excessive cost outlay, foolish investments or poor margins that will be detrimental to the family's wealth.

The opposite extreme – where all the board members are independent non-executive directors – is equally undesirable. The great danger with a board made up in this way is that it will be too distant from the running of the enterprise and may not have a very good understanding of the challenges and issues. Those directors will be entirely dependent on what management serves up to them and may soon discover that all the subjects passed to them for decision have been 'pre-cooked'. There might well be three options on the table from which to choose but there'll usually be one that's obviously better than the others and comes with the recommendation of the management, so that basically there's no real freedom of decision.

The best situation from a role-distribution point of view is when non-independent, independent, executive and non-executive directors are sitting on the board. How many directors in each category you should have will depend on the specific circumstances and the desired total size of the board. Legal provisions and regulations will obviously also matter. Belgian law lays down how many independent directors there should be and how long their mandate should be. There's also a legal definition of what 'independent director' means. Traditionally, and also as required by law in Belgium, the chief executive officer and all members of the executive board of banking institutions also sit on the board of directors. At non-banking firms, this rule generally applies only to the CEO. Sometimes the CFO also sits on the board but often in an observer capacity or in order to draw up the minutes of the meeting.

The great advantage of having executive directors on the governing body is that this enables direct, face-to-face encounters between executives and the non-executive directors. Moreover, it's often preferable that these encounters don't only involve the CEO, so that the other top executives are not dependent on a single source of information and can obtain a more comprehensive view of how things are going at the company and at the governing body. However, even if several other executives sit on the board alongside the CEO, that still doesn't necessarily mean that the non-executive directors are going to hear a variety of opinions, as the chief executive will usually try to ensure that everyone is singing from the same hymn sheet and toeing the same line. This won't be a problem, at least not if the non-executive directors remain alert to any signs that indicate differences of opinion or indeed to any other insights. This will also help the directors to judge whether the CEO still has the support of his team. Moreover,

If one manager is given a board seat while others are not, this may arouse resentment.

they'll get to know the other senior managers and begin to form an opinion as to who might be able to head up the company in the future. There are thus a number of advantages in having several executives sitting on the board of directors, although most CEOs prefer to be the only one as this will make for less friction. It is, moreover, the case that if some managers are given board seats while others are not, this can cause resentment.

Executive directors often make a valuable addition to the board, especially if they're also shareholders in the firm. Clearly their equity interest will be aligned with the company's results and risks. They may also be in a position to give some indications of what will be feasible for shareholders in terms of financing future capital investment and what the dividend policy should be. In addition, they may be able to provide useful input when it comes to the appointment and appraisal of management.

Trade unions, NGOs and other pressure groups

A debate has been going on for a long time about whether or not trade unions or other workforce representatives ought to have seats on company boards, as is the case for instance in Germany. Some company bosses think this would be a good thing, as employees would then have a clearer grasp of the challenges facing businesses and get a better idea of why particular decisions have been made. This also means that employees would be involved in the decisions taken and so become more ready to support those decisions.

Other company bosses fear that the presence of employees on the board will lead to a de facto split in the boardroom and that every debate on an important issue will be referred to small reflection groups that will then force their preferred course of action on to the full board. The problem is less acute in Belgium because the trade unions, as workforce representatives, generally prefer not to be part of company boards so as to avoid being directly implicated in the company's policies. This does not, however, exclude the possibility of trade unions sitting on boards as social organisations. So the debate on this question is not yet over.

In future we can expect all kinds of pressure groups, such as NGOs, to argue that they should have representation on company governing bodies. We already saw this when the peace movement was raising issues regarding certain products made by the Flemish technology group Barco. At that time there were already calls for the peace movement and civil society to be given a seat on the Barco board. The appointee would logically have been a non-independent director, given that s/he would clearly be representing a particular interest, in the same way as shareholders do.

I'm not a great advocate of direct representation for NGOs on the boards of limited liability companies, whether listed or unlisted, as this tends to distort the decision-making process. To me, it seems more logical that each party should take a viewpoint on a given issue and then negotiations could perhaps take place. Nonetheless, I predict that in the future, stock exchange-listed firms will in any case co-opt more independent directors who are in touch with society at large and the NGO world. Moreover, businesses will certainly become more aware of their social and environmental responsibilities.

EXPERTISE

The expertise of individual directors plays a part in deciding the composition of a board. In order to carry out its duties properly, the board of directors must be able to draw on a variety of skills. The precise range of skills required varies from company to company, from organisation to organisation and from sector to sector so I can't provide an exhaustive list here. Going on my own experience, however, I think the following skills will be useful in every case: sector knowledge and strategic insight as regards the sector, the markets and the competition; knowledge of finance and of how the financial markets work and react; knowledge of the local, European and also, where necessary, the international legislative and regulatory framework; insight into social change; insight into customer behaviour; insight into employee expectations and also how to make up for any shortage in trained staff; knowledge and insight into technological developments, especially digitalisation; a good grasp of logistical processes; experience with the processes of internationalisation and company transformation; plus a broad network of social and political contacts. This is a fairly long list but I could easily have made it twice as long.

Of course, you can't expect to appoint a separate director for each particular area of expertise. The governing body would then have to be much too big. Moreover, you would then have a collection of experts sitting next to each other who wouldn't necessarily make up a team. It's a much better idea to bring together a group of intelligent people who possess both business sense and common sense plus some specific skills such as the ones I've described above. A leading expert in a given field who's incapable of making useful input to a decision-making process where other kinds of expertise are important is likely to bring very little added value to a board of directors.

There are other disadvantages to having top experts who lack common sense and a general understanding sitting on a board of directors. Very often they're rather reluctant to take part in the board debates. They may even pose a threat to the experts in their particular field who are working at the company because this kind of director will want to show that s/he's the cleverest person around.

This is why I'm not in favour of filling the board with human resources, digitalisation or audit and risk specialists. In themselves, these are of course very important fields, but in the board of directors, it's first and foremost about reaching a sensible, well-thought-out decision in the best interests of the company and of the various parties involved with the company. Specialist expertise is needed, but so are a range of other skills that will help the board to make wise, prudent collective decisions. To make a slightly offbeat comparison, there's a huge difference between a board of directors, which collectively weighs and sizes things up, and the panel of judges for an ice-skating competition, where each judge individually holds up a board with a score assessing the performance of each skater. A company board wouldn't be able to work according to this kind of rigid 'box-ticking' approach, which is not at all conducive to carefully-considered, creative decisions.

GENDER DIVERSITY

A third element in the composition of the board of directors is the gender balance. In 2012, following legislative initiatives in other European countries, Belgium passed a law stipulating that at least one third of the directors of a stock exchange-listed company must be men or women. In spite of considerable hesitation over the entry into force of this rule, nearly all listed Belgian companies made the necessary adaptation on time. Gender diversity is indeed necessary, not because it improves company performance but because this is part and parcel of women's rights. Nowadays, companies have a much stronger female presence, the clientele has strong female influence, and society as a whole is much more gender-balanced than before. Consequently, this should also be the case for company boards. I have personally taken active steps to help improve the gender balance on a number of boards, even before the new law was passed. I've always seen this as the right way to go.

Nevertheless, I have some reservations about the precise way the gender balance requirement has been formulated in the new legislation. The one-third rule lays down a general requirement but nothing is said about how board seats should be allocated to various kinds of directors – independent, non-independent, executive and non-executive. The outcome of this is that now more women are occupying 'independent' board seats in Belgium. However, there has for many years been a shortage of women in management positions who are thus eligible to serve as executive directors and, at the same time, there's a shortage of women among shareholders, i.e. the people who usually appoint the non-independent directors. Sometimes this deficiency will be unavoidable as family shareholdings will be represented by a family member and you can't always insist on gender diversity in such cases. There are of course exceptions, such as the family-owned companies Sioen, Reynaers and ETAP. But it would have been better to set a quota, to be followed every time a new director is to be elected. This would have meant that the gender balance could be improved across all categories of director.

Factor 4 Governance model

The fourth factor determining the context within which board directors perform their duties is the chosen governance model. As I very briefly mentioned in Chapter 1, there are basically two governance models: the one-tier board and the two-tier board. The two-tier model is the easiest to explain; it then becomes obvious what 'one-tier' means.

Under the two-tier system, which has been in operation for many years in Germany and the Netherlands, there is clear separation between the executive and supervisory roles. There's a purely supervisory body, which is known in Germany as the *Aufsichtsrat* (literally: Oversight Council) and in the Netherlands as the *Raad van Commissarissen* (Council of Commissioners). Then there's an executive board, which is responsible for both initiating policies and strategies and decision-making. In Germany, this body bears the name *Vorstand* (derived from a verb meaning to lead, head up or preside) and in the Netherlands is called the *Raad van Bestuur* (literally: Management Council). As this is precisely the name used in the Flemish-speaking part of Belgium for the one-tier board of directors, the terminology can cause some confusion among Belgian and Dutch businesspeople and shareholders. The name used to describe a member of the board of directors in Belgium is the same as that used in the neighbouring country for a member of the executive body who has a direct hands-on role in the day-to-day running of the company.

Germany and the Netherlands are the most prominent European countries to have opted for the 'split board' approach. Meanwhile, firms in the English-speaking countries continue to operate under a one-tier governance system.

In Belgium, lawyers, academics and some shareholders were calling repeatedly over many years for the introduction of a two-tier system and the law now provides this option. Nevertheless, very few companies have actually chosen to go that route. There is certainly considerable reluctance to do so among shareholders who are closely involved with their company, as they fear that this approach will distance them from the enterprise and prevent them from maintaining a good grasp of how the management are running the business. Supervision is in fact a kind of *ex-post* control. The company management take an initiative, get it running and then the oversight commissioners, or whatever they're called, pass judgement on it. If things go badly wrong, you can of course replace the management. However, at family firms or companies with a strong, competent, reference shareholder, the shareholders will certainly prefer to exercise *ex-ante* control. With this approach, the management are expected to explain in advance what they are planning to do so that the governing body can give its opinion and have the opportunity to approve or reject the plans.

> In Belgium, shareholders haven't shown much interest in a split-governance model.

Nor is it only shareholders who have doubts about the two-tier model; I've often heard managers express reservations as well. Under the two-tier system, decision-making is based on a collegial approach and the chief executive officer is usually *primus inter pares* on the board of management or executive board. It is, moreover, based on collective responsibility. Not all managers like this, nor is it always to the taste of the CEO, who would usually much rather keep a firm grip on decision-making. For all these reasons, the two-tier model doesn't have many supporters among either shareholders or management.

In any case, the benefits of this model are not so great as to make it clearly superior to the one-tier approach. One advantage of the two-tier model that people like to point to is that it makes it harder to take the company over. Because of the sharp division between execution and supervision, the acquirer cannot simply seize hold of the management of the company just like that. However, this is probably no long-term advantage, as it's likely to lead to conflict between the shareholders on the one side and the management on the other. There's also a risk that the management will become lax in its running of the business and will sometimes fail to take the necessary steps to keep the enterprise on a successful path.

Fortunately, the Belgian legislators have given company shareholders the freedom to choose for themselves the governance model which the shareholders and management think offers the best chance of building a stable and successful business. However, banks don't have this freedom because a form of two-tier governance for the Belgian banking sector was introduced way back in the 1930s.

In short, directors ('commissioners' is the chosen term in some places) operating under a two-tier governance system have a different sort of task and will clearly have to work in a different manner than their colleagues who are operating under a one-tier system.

Factor 5 Delegation to management

The fifth factor is the tasks and responsibilities that are delegated to management. The board of directors is supposed to do everything necessary to achieve the purpose or object of the company or organisation, but that is of course not feasible. The activities and duties to be performed are too numerous, too complex, too time-consuming and too repetitive for the board to accomplish all by itself. The directors therefore delegate a range of tasks to the executive management and staff. This enables the organisation to function independently within a certain framework and decisions don't necessarily have to receive the prior approval of the governing body, although the directors will subsequently assess the decisions taken and the results posted and pass judgement on them as necessary. Meanwhile, the management will in any case be empowered to take the day-to-day decisions.

But what exactly do we mean by day-to-day decisions? In a chemicals company, investing in a new plant can hardly be described as part of day-to-day decision-making, whereas at a private equity firm investing is of course the investment managers' daily bread and butter. This sort of problem is usually solved in one of two ways. The first way is to empower the management to take and implement decisions that are part and parcel of the approved company strategy up to a certain level of expenditure. Prior approval will not be necessary but there will be an *ex post* assessment. The second way is to allow the management to fulfil any commitments that were included in the previously approved budget. The budget thus becomes a sort of contract between the board and the management, whereby the management say what they intend to spend in order to achieve the targets set. If the directors approve the proposed budget, this implies delegating to management the power to execute the plans. Anything not provided for in the budget, such as a takeover bid, will have to be sent back up to the board. The same goes in cases where the budget wasn't very precise about a new investment or fresh expenditure.

Of course, the power to represent the company and make commitments on its behalf must also be delegated. Such delegated powers may be set out in a rider to the statutes, and subject to regular reconfirmation. It's of fundamental importance to all concerned – directors, management and third parties – that formal instruments of delegation actually exist and that they are absolutely clear.

The powers delegated to management can be either quite extensive or more circumscribed. Once again, we should underline here that the duties and way of working of the board of directors will be determined by the way in which and the extent to which such powers are delegated.

Factor 6 The legal & regulatory framework and social responsibility

What is expected of the directors also depends on the legal and regulatory framework and the social responsibility which the company or organisation is willing to assume. This is the sixth factor determining the context in which the governing body has to do its work.

LEGISLATION AND REGULATION

It's perfectly obvious that a board of directors must work within the legal and regulatory framework in force. This hardly needs any extra explanation. It's important to point out, however, that the legal requirements are not identical for every board. Different requirements are placed upon a stock exchange-listed company as regards the composition of the board and financial communication than on unlisted enterprises. The requirement regarding the appointment of independent directors also differs from company to company as does the length of their mandates. Consequently, directors need to pay attention to specific legislation that may be applicable to their board.

Banks are a typical example. Banking legislation and the regulations that have applied to banks and their governing bodies ever since the financial crisis are very extensive, very specific and extremely binding. Bank directors must exercise supervision over the risks that the bank is taking and have now also taken on considerable responsibility regarding the remuneration and bonuses paid to bank employees. These duties are not of central importance for boards in other sectors. At most types of companies, shareholders are free to choose whom they wish to elect as directors, providing at least that they comply with the gender balance requirements. This is not the case for banks, where every director must obtain the approval of the European Central Bank before s/he can be finally appointed by the AGM. In some countries, they're now talking about formal certification for bank directors, or even for company directors in general. I don't think this is a very good idea as it will probably add a layer of unnecessary bureaucracy to the process of appointing board members, who will then tend to become inspectors, focusing hard on the rules but making very little contribution to the company's business performance. This doesn't seem to me to be the right way to go at a time when we're experiencing what is probably the greatest technological upheaval in corporate history.

Regulations also vary from sector to sector and company to company. It's clear that directors must abide by the regulations and see to it that their company follows the rules. This is why compliance has become so important at all kinds of enterprises.

SOCIAL RESPONSIBILITY

However, there is more than just the legislative and regulatory framework to be taken into account. These days, directors and the board as a whole must be aware that the company also has a responsibility to society. Let me stress once again: on this front, one company is not the same as another and not all governing bodies approach their social responsibility in exactly the same way. There is however no longer any doubt that such responsibility exists and that they need to take it on board.

I'd like to repeat here the rather provocative title of an article that Nobel prize winner Milton Friedman wrote almost forty years ago: "The social responsibility of business is to increase profits". That statement is no longer acceptable – at least not in this simplistic formulation. However, if you re-read the original article, it's clear that Friedman was not actually making such a simplistic claim. He was only drawing attention to the fact that a company ought not to misuse shareholders' assets in order to take on a missionary role.

In recent years, it has become clear that a company which takes no account of the wellbeing of its customers and suppliers and also the environment is more likely to destroy than create value for its shareholders. The examples are numerous. Volkswagen lost a significant part of its stock market value when it came to light that the company had been cheating on the testing of harmful emissions from its vehicles. Food companies have lost market value because doubts arose over the safety of their products. Clothing firms have been held accountable for the origin of the clothes they sell. Nowadays, it's perfectly clear that directors must see to it that their company follows sustainable policies. The exact requirements will vary from one type of business to another but the directors must be prepared to take steps to ensure that the management pursues a sustainable strategy. This is in the best interests of the company, the shareholders and the workforce, and above all of the wider society.

Factor 7 Personal characteristics of the directors and managers

The seventh and final factor determining the context in which the governing body carries out its duties is the personal characteristics of the directors and managers. If this seems surprising, I should perhaps point out again that the tasks which the board of directors has to accomplish are not set in stone. What board members have to do depends, as we've already seen above, on a number of factors, but much also depends on the individuals who are doing the jobs of directors and managers. Are they prepared to work together to find solutions to the problems that arise? Do they trust each other? Will they listen to each other? If not, then corporate governance will become simply a matter of sticking rigidly to rules and regulations but not really looking into what ought to be happening at the company. Personal egos can easily get in the way of running the company. They can lead to epic battles between the chair and the CEO and between the board of directors and

> Personal egos can easily get in the way of running the company.

the executive board. Battles of this kind are of no benefit whatsoever to the company, its customers or its employees. Such tensions and quarrels will even threaten the very survival of the company. I'll come back to this point later in the book.

Temporary and incidental factors

I've described above the structural elements that determine the context within which a board of directors and its constituent members has to perform its core duties. Those structural elements will determine whether the directors focus primarily on supervision and monitoring or whether they are also involved in setting the course for the organisation. The structural elements are of vital importance in determining context. Nevertheless, a number of temporary or incidental factors may also have an impact.

If a company gets into financial difficulties because a strategic plan fails, either due to a serious slump in turnover, fierce competition, a change in consumer behaviour or extreme fluctuations in the currency exchange rates vis-à-vis its export markets, the governing body will need to take on a different role. First and foremost, board meetings will usually take place more frequently. Instead of the usual four to six meetings a year, the board will perhaps have to meet every month or more often. In the first place, the directors' supervision and monitoring tasks will increase; subsequently they will need to place more emphasis on the course-setting aspect of their role.

If it turns out that the financial problems are in fact due to fraudulent activity, the governing body – or at least some members of the board – will become closely involved in the day-to-day hands-on management of the company.

A problem may also arise if it becomes apparent that the CEO or the management are not able to find the right solutions to the challenges facing the company. At that moment the governing body will have to decide whether to replace the CEO and/or the management. This is a very delicate issue that needs to be approached with great care. I'll come back to this issue in a moment.

To sum up

There's no such thing as a one-size-fits-all 'board of directors'. In this chapter, I've shown how every governing body differs from all the others. This is because each board of directors has to work within a context that differs from company to company or from organisation to organisation. The most important factor determining the context is the shareholder structure. In every case, the governing body will differ according to the differences in shareholder structure. In addition to such elements as the governance model and the powers and responsibilities delegated by the directors to the management, another important factor is the personalities of the top people in the company or organisation. I'll go into this point more deeply in the following pages.

CHAPTER 3

The building blocks of a governing body

What you need in order to assemble a board of directors

A governing body is made up of six structural elements. It's often said that the structure determines whether or not a board of directors will work well. This is partly true. Also important, however, is how the directors conduct themselves within that structure. In this chapter, we'll focus on the six building blocks. We'll take a look at the behaviour of the chairman or woman and the other members of the board in the following chapters.

THE SIX ELEMENTS FROM WHICH THE GOVERNING BODY OF A FOR-profit company or organisation without profit motive is made up are: the composition of the board of directors; the number of committees reporting to the board and their specific duties; the particular way the board works; the rules of the game and the conduct of the directors sitting on the board; liaison and cooperation between the board and the management team; and lastly the board chairman or woman. I'll explain all these points in detail in this chapter and I'll go on to say more about these building blocks later in the book.

Building block 1 Composition of the board of directors

What size should a board of directors be? I can answer this question in a rather simplistic, but not inaccurate, way: as small as possible (in accordance with the legal requirements, of course) and as large as necessary. This calls for some clarification. A board should preferably be as small as possible so that its meetings can be run efficiently. It's much easier to call a small board together than a large one because there will be fewer diary clashes to resolve. Moreover, if a board meeting lasts for, say, 150 minutes, there will of course be more speaking time for every director if there are only six of them around the table than if fifteen are taking part. If there are a lot of points on the agenda and the board is quite large, the

> The larger the board, the harder it will be to reach a consensus.

contribution from each director may be almost negligible. So it's far from easy to have an in-depth discussion – or to reach consensus – on every point in a very large board of directors. Nevertheless, it is sometimes useful or actually necessary to have a large board, as I'll explain in the next section.

The size of a board of directors will depend mainly on the different types of directors who are sitting around the table. These types include executive directors (usually the chief executive officer plus several members of the management committee) and non-executive directors. Among non-executive directors, we should differentiate between independent and non- independent directors. Independent directors will not possess any significant shareholding in the business and will not be sitting as a representative of any large shareholder. Non-independent directors will be representing large shareholders or may themselves actually have a sizeable stake in the company. Such representatives may in fact be employees or former employees of a major shareholder.

There may be a large number of executive directors sitting on the board. In Belgium, this is usually the case with banks, where four or five of the directors will have hands-on management jobs. At other types of company or non-profit organisation, only the chief executive officer (CEO) will be a member or acting member of the board, sometimes supported by the chief financial officer (CFO). There are also instances where the CEO isn't actually an appointed member of the board of directors but is nevertheless invited to attend all its meetings.

The number of executive directors will have a direct impact on the number of non-executive and non-independent directors appointed to the board. In all cases, the major shareholders will – for obvious reasons – always seek to ensure that directors representing those shareholders are in the majority. So if there are various different blocks of shareholders requiring board representation, the total number of directors can quickly escalate.

As I indicated above, board meetings where the number of sitting directors is large are likely to be less efficient. Meetings may have to run for longer or with fewer points on the agenda, in which case the frequency of meetings may have to increase. However, the advantage of a large board, especially at a company or organisation where different blocks of shareholders or interested stakeholders are involved, is of course that all the various points of view can be voiced at the meetings. The more viewpoints that are expressed, the more any given decision will reflect the interests of all those involved, though with the attendant risk that collective decision-making becomes more difficult. If however the interests of all the shareholders converge, the decision-making process is likely to go smoothly.

An example of this is a technology company where a number of venture capital firms hold stakes in the enterprise and are represented on the board of directors. All shareholders have an interest in seeing the value of the business rise rapidly so that the company can be floated on the stock exchange and they can make a return on their investment.

Non-executive directors who represent one or more major shareholders should of course bear in mind that they're supposed to be acting in the best interests of the company and all its shareholders. If necessary, the independent directors should serve as a counterweight so as to safeguard the interests of those shareholders who are not represented on the board.

Building block 2 **Committees**

The second element on which a board of directors is built is its committees. Most committees have official recognition and are also recommended by the corporate governance codes or the law, as is the case with banks. These include the audit committee, the risk committee, the remuneration committee and the appointments committee. Committees may also be set up to work on governance, strategy and the prevention of conflicts of interest. Personally I don't think it's very useful to set up a strategy committee, as this will remove an important subject from the remit of the board itself or will result in less importance being given to the subject at board meetings, when in fact company strategy is one of the most important subjects that the board has to consider. In fact, very often the reason why a strategy committee is set up is that major shareholders would rather discuss strategy proposals among themselves before submitting them to the full board.

To enable committees to work properly, there are a number of things that need to be settled in advance. You need to appoint a chair and several members. However, the composition of some or all the board committees will already be determined by legislation or regulation. There must always be independent directors on the committee. This might mean that you need to increase the number of independent directors on the board, especially if you wish to avoid a situation where some independent directors are sitting on several different committees – which will basically mean having a larger board. This shows yet again that you can't just decide in advance on a given number of directors for the board. Everything will depend on the number of tasks that need to be performed and on the balance of power in the boardroom.

After appointing the chair and the other members of each committee, you will need to draw up charters containing instructions for the workings of each committee, which will then have to be approved by the governing body. In order to convey their findings on the various subjects entrusted to them back to the full board, each committee will need to draw up well-formulated reports. Only after the board has taken note of proposals made by the committee can a final decision be recorded. Each of these committees can therefore be regarded as an advisory body for the board of directors, although the board might decide to formally delegate part of its authority to a committee. In my opinion, this practice should remain the exception rather than the rule. In cases where legislation or regulations are able to exert influence in this area, they usually don't condone this approach.

Building block 3 **The workings of the board**

In Chapter 4, I'll discuss in detail issues around the agenda for board meetings and the workings of the board. I'll therefore restrict myself here to just mentioning two aspects of importance: the frequency of board meetings and the flow of information.

In principle, it's not necessary to lay down precisely how often the board of directors should meet, apart from where there are specific legal prescriptions. It's probably advisable for large boards to meet more often, each time with a manageable agenda so that the directors can have their say about each item. Smaller boards can probably meet less often and deal with longer agendas. It's good practice to set a fixed meeting date, so that the meeting can be planned properly and board members can mark their diaries. Any director who is persistently absent from board meetings should be unseated.

It's important to ensure a good flow of information, so good reporting is essential, with decisions precisely minuted and a clear distinction made between what was discussed and what was actually decided. In the United States, the common practice is to turn the minutes of the meeting into a legal document in which all board decisions are set out. In Belgium, the meeting secretary endeavours, in addition, to accurately reflect the considerations and debates that led to each particular decision. Sometimes directors like to have their remarks recorded by name, though I'm doubtful that this is good practice in normal situations, as it's quite likely to lead to some degree of 'egotripping'.

Building block 4 **Rules of the game, conduct and meetings culture**

Some, though not all, governing bodies draw up a code of conduct for the directors. The main emphasis here is usually on the need to provide honest, trustworthy information. The code will also forbid any misuse of information in order to obtain an advantage on the market or the stock exchange. It will also stipulate when and how directors or their family members may trade in the company's equity or the shares of related firms. The behaviour expected of directors vis-à-vis customers and suppliers will also be set out in the code of conduct.

What is less often formally regulated, but may be established through good practice, is the firm's meetings culture. It's important that directors should feel that they can discuss things openly in the boardroom and ask any questions they wish. The CEO and the managers are also expected to go along with this culture of openness. I've learned that the effectiveness of a director in a discussion largely depends on the way questions are put. Directors who frame their questions in an arrogant, smug manner often find out much less than those who cleverly formulate questions in a seemingly innocent way. To a very large extent, the chair sets the tone. If s/he encourages directors to ask questions and gives them the time to do so, this attitude will help to create a positive meetings culture. Ignoring directors or not letting them get a word in edgeways is not a very useful way to run board meetings.

Under the heading 'rules of the game, conduct and meetings culture' I would also include an appraisal of the board of directors, i.e. an annual assessment of how well the board has been working, which should be discussed in a collegial, self-critical manner. This can help to improve the board's meetings culture. Some companies and organisations call upon an external consultant to run the appraisal process, while others prefer to do it themselves. I don't think one way is necessarily better than the other.

Building block 5 Liaison between board and management

Directors occasionally need to put questions or make comments directly to managers outside the official meetings. They have not only a perfect right, but also the obligation, to do so if they feel that something is going wrong or if they believe that they possess information, knowledge or expertise which a manager will find useful. However, in such cases the director must take care to avoid creating parallel channels which will sideline the chief executive officer. It's therefore good practice to keep both the CEO and the chairperson informed about any such steps taken. There must also be no doubt as to who is the direct superior of the manager with whom the director has got in touch: in every case this is the CEO; the director must not do anything to give the impression that s/he sees him/herself as a sort of 'superboss'. Directors are not entitled to give direct orders to management, just to provide advice. It's also a good idea to remember that unsolicited advice is rarely effective. It's usually better to wait for a request for advice.

> A director mustn't try to play the role of 'überboss'.

Directors should of course abandon this prudent approach if the company or organisation is clearly in crisis. Even then however, a coordinated approach by the chair and the board members, perhaps in conjunction with the CEO – if s/he's still in post – is preferable to an individual initiative by one single director.

Building block 6 **The chair**

The final important element for assembling a governing body is the appointment of a chairman or woman. At companies with a highly fragmented shareholder structure, the sitting directors usually elect one of their number to chair the board. At firms with one dominant shareholder or several major shareholder blocks, the shareholders will designate the chairperson. Sometimes the shareholders strike a formal agreement about the chairmanship. It often happens that the dominant shareholder will take the chair him/herself. There's nothing wrong with this in itself, since the dominant shareholder certainly has an interest in ensuring that the company performs well. Nevertheless, conflicts of interest may arise if the reference shareholder is also invested in other companies. In such cases, the other shareholders have a duty to monitor the situation.

I'll go into detail on the role of the chair of a governing body in a later chapter. I'll confine myself here to underlining that the chairperson must above all ensure that the board takes account, in a fair and balanced manner, of the interests of all involved parties.

To sum up

A governing body will only work properly if it's built on a solid structure. In this chapter, I've described the various elements that make up this structure. I've nevertheless discovered that a good structure is not in itself sufficient to ensure that a governing body will work well. Of at least equal importance is the conduct of the directors. To give a simple example, you can't be sure that a city with an excellent transport infrastructure will not have any traffic accidents unless the drivers using the infrastructure drive their vehicles carefully and are aware of their responsibilities. It's the combination of the right structure and the right behaviour that will help the governing body to do its job properly.

CHAPTER 4

The meeting agenda

What directors come together to talk about

What sort of items will be on the boardroom table? On what subjects will the directors take real decisions? Or are they basically there to approve proposals from the management? Which agenda points are only there for information?

IN CARRYING OUT ITS WORK, THE GOVERNING BODY'S MOST IMPORTANT tool is the meeting agenda. Apart from that, there's usually a to-do list, but this normally contains subjects, issues and points that have come up during discussions between the directors or with management and have not yet found their way on to the agenda but may subsequently be placed on the agenda for debate at a subsequent meeting. The agenda is the true guideline for the work performed by the board of directors.

Board meetings without an agenda don't really enable the directors to carry out their core duties, as I've described them in Chapter 1, properly. Nevertheless, it can make sense to hold a short meeting without a formal agenda. In fact, quite a lot of governing bodies hold a meeting once a year without the CEO or other management personnel present in order to exchange ideas on how things are going. This basically provides an opportunity for directors to express their thoughts freely about the nuts and bolts of the company or organisation. I don't mean to suggest that this should be a sort of secret gathering of directors. It is in fact preferable to inform the CEO and the management in a fully transparent way that this meeting is taking place and the management should perhaps also be subsequently informed about what went on at this agenda-free session. However, holding this kind of meeting gives directors the chance to reflect freely about how things are going at the company or organisation, how the management is doing and how the board itself is performing. The advantage of holding this kind of 'directors-only' session regularly – perhaps once a year – is that it will not be viewed as out of the ordinary and so will be less likely to arouse suspicions between the CEO, the management and the non-executive directors.

In principle, it should be possible to place any subject at all on the board's meeting agenda. This follows logically from the principle that the board of directors is basically responsible for everything and is supposed to do everything necessary to achieve the company's purpose and objectives. Nevertheless, it makes sense to concentrate on governance issues. Executive-related subjects and items that are strictly operational or highly detailed in nature should preferably not be placed on the board's agenda. Directors are not the right people to deliver judgement or make choices between possible options in the executive or operational domain.

In practice, we can differentiate between points that appear on the agenda for virtually every meeting and other points that are more usually discussed on a quarterly, half-yearly or even annual basis. Certain items will return to the agenda with absolute regularity, while other points will be discussed more exceptionally.

The table above gives an overview of the subjects and items that may appear on the agenda for governing body meetings. It also provides an indication of how frequently various different points are addressed at the meetings. The frequency also of course depends on the context within which the board of directors is working – at a listed company, an unlisted, closed corporation, and so on. In the last column, I've indicated the type of action that directors will be expected to undertake. Practically all items should be prepared and tabled for board discussion by the chief executive officer and the management. The directors will then be expected to take note of the papers tabled and question the management about their contents. When necessary, they will approve the papers, in other cases it will suffice simply to take cognisance of them.

It's useful to differentiate between approval and collective decision. By 'approval' I mean that the board does not have exclusive jurisdiction over the matters pertaining to the agenda item. Management asks for the board's approval in order to strengthen its position vis-à-vis the

Frequency of item on the agenda	Subjects that appear on the board meeting agenda	Concrete agenda items	Action expected from the directors
Rarely on the agenda but of far-reaching impact	1 Corporate vision and purpose	· Long-term aims and objectives of the company/ organisation · Corporate values	· Task the management to come up with proposals · Question the management
	2 Operations and behaviour	· Policy on specific aspects such as: preventing conflicts of interest, ethical conduct, policy on relationships with competitors · Key procedures · Approval of delegation and proxies	· Task the management to take initiatives · Take note of existing initiatives · Put questions and grant approval · Monitor compliance
	3 Sale of the company; takeover bid on the company	· Discussion and, if appropriate, action to facilitate the sale; assessment of the company valuation (bid price) · Independent assessment of the bid	· Discuss with management · Draw up proposals for the shareholders
Not very frequent	4 Strategy	· Approval, assessment, adjustment of company strategy · Discussion of strategy for particular sets of products, activities and markets; business/ earnings models · Technology developments · Digitalisation · Competitor analysis	· Question the management · Grant approval · Take decision to make adjustments
	5 Mergers and acquisitions	· Proposals for mergers and acquisitions	· Question the management · Take decision
	6 Governance	· New board members/renewal of sitting directors' mandates · Assessment of the board's performance · Composition of committees · Conflicts of interest	· Take decision
	7 Leadership (some aspects appear quite often on the board-room table, others less frequently)	· Recruitment · Appraisals · Remuneration/compensation policy for top management · Variable compensation · Dismissals	· Question the management · Draw up proposals for shareholders when necessary · Take decisions

Frequent	8 Shareholder relations	· Annual accounts and annual report · Information for investors and analysts · Agenda and preparations for AGM/EGM · Press releases	· Grant approval · Draw up proposals for shareholders · Take decisions
	9 Stakeholder relations	· Customer satisfaction · Regulators and public authorities · Compliance · Relations with trade unions · Interest groups	· Question the management · Take note
	10 Employee relations	· HR policy · Monitoring available skills/expertise · Employee satisfaction · Burn-out/Employee wellbeing · Work accidents	· Question the management · Take note
	11 Results	· Actual business/financial results · Results forecast · Benchmarking	· Question the management · Take note
	12 Risks	· Financial risks/other risks · Risk appetite · Cybersecurity	· Question the management · Take note · Take decisions
	13 Financing	· Budgeting · Forecast · Financial structure · Dividends · Capital increase · Share buy-back · Loans · Ratings · Provisions for future commitments	· Question the management · Take note · Grant approval · Take decisions

Agenda items for meetings of the board of directors

organisation and the outside world. When I say 'collective decision', I'm referring to subjects and specific points over which the board does have explicit jurisdiction, although of course it will still be the CEO or other management personnel who prepare the ground for the decision.

It also happens that certain points, such as for example the size of the dividend to be distributed, the appointment of directors, renewal of a director's mandate or a merger proposal, may require a formal decision at the AGM. In these cases, it's up to the directors to take a collective decision as to the exact proposal that will be put to the shareholders.

It's not really possible to specify for every agenda item whether the board's task is precisely a matter of course-setting or of supervision at that particular company or organisation. Nearly all agenda items comprise both aspects. A good example of this is the task of approving the budget. On the one hand, the budget sets the course for the enterprise in that it lays down the amount of company resources that can be spent during the following year. On the other hand, the budget is a tool or yardstick with which directors are able to exercise supervision of the organisation, i.e. by examining what has been done with the company resources and assessing how the business has prospered as a result.

In the following pages, I'll discuss the meeting agenda subject-by-subject or point-by-point and now and then I'll stop to dissect a specific agenda item. Each description will give an idea of the kind of thing that might land on the boardroom table. The reader will notice that the list of potential subjects is rather extensive; yet it's still not complete. Points can always appear on the board agenda on subjects not mentioned here, such as for instance a major lawsuit, a shareholder initiative or a campaign by activists. I've pointed out several times already that the governing body has a legal obligation to do everything necessary to enable the company to achieve its purpose and objectives. It should therefore not be surprising that the list of subjects and points is rather extensive and can basically never be exhaustive. It's very hard to predict what exactly will be required in order to 'do everything necessary'.

It goes without saying that a governing body which only meets four times a year will not be able to deal with all subjects and points. However, you don't in fact have to deal with every subject every year. The board ought to be able to touch on all necessary subjects over a period of three to four years.

Setting out a corporate vision

The most important thing that a board of directors is supposed to do (but doesn't always do) is to set out a vision and purpose for the company or organisation. The corporate vision is basically *what* the company or organisation endeavours to be or to become, while the purpose describes *why* it's seeking to attain that vision. Sometimes the expression 'vision' might be replaced by the word 'ambition'. I'll give a couple of examples to try to make these expressions clearer.

An investment company may have a vision of transforming itself into a private equity firm that mainly takes minority stakes in industrial companies in a number of European countries. It might alternatively decide to concentrate exclusively on buy-outs in certain European countries. In order to do so, it might set up a local investment team in all the countries where it does business. To finance its investment activities, it might want to attract closed fund capital from pension funds or funds of funds. Another possibility is to raise capital through a stock exchange listing, as a number of private equity firms in several European countries have done. This example demonstrates that the 'vision' of an investment company may vary across a range and so choices will have to be made: I've mentioned only a few here. One of the key tasks of a board of directors is to formulate an answer to the question: "*What is the company's vision (or ambition)?*".

Then there's the purpose of the company: why does the company wish to pursue one or the other vision? Once again taking the example of our investment company, several answers are possible. The purpose might be to ensure as high and stable a return as possible for the shareholders. Alternatively, the firm might define its purpose as contributing to overall economic growth by supporting growth at the various businesses in which it invests. Each of these two purposes would call for a different approach, although it's still of course a fact that if the board opts for the second purpose, they won't be able to achieve it unless the firm makes a decent return.

A second example is Barco, a Belgian technology company that has built up a world-class position with advanced projection systems for cinemas and other high-value applications where image definition, clarity, reliability and connectivity are key. Barco has also set up other divisions, including healthcare and control systems, in each case targeting the professional user. Apart from some cautious forays into the audio market, which have generally not been a success, Barco has remained focused on various niches in the video market. This is an example of a clear corporate vision. However, the purpose might be one of several. Is the company striving for technological leadership or instead looking to maximise company value? Once again, these two purposes are mutually linked. However, going for maximum company value might mean that they will occasionally have to take a step backwards in their drive for technological leadership as the search for leadership in this field may call for capital investment that will only pay off in the very long term, resulting in a lower company value today. These are choices which a board of directors makes either explicitly or implicitly.

> Growth or return on investment? It's up to the directors to choose.

Purpose

Like many other concept words, the term 'purpose' may carry a range
of meanings. In a narrow business context, we may think of this as basically referring to a company's overall objectives or numerical targets.
However, the word does contain a more general or moral sense: what
drives the company? What does the company stand for? Or a highly
personal notion in relation to the employees: what gets you out of bed in
the morning and propels you out of the door and off to work? And if the
answer is simply "to earn money", there's no shame in that.

However, it's now becoming increasingly necessary to motivate
staff and also to ensure that the company plays an acceptable role
in the wider society. Nowadays people would much rather work for a
company that endeavours to make a meaningful contribution to society
through its products, its customer care, the way in which it produces
and delivers its goods and services and the way it interacts with the
environment and impacts our climate.

Corporate vision and purpose are not short-term matters. The company's vision and purpose should set the course for the organisation
in the long term. Determining the corporate vision is therefore not
a task that will regularly reappear on the board's meeting agenda.
However, it's very rare that the corporate vision can be determined 'in
a single shot'. Usually, it will grow and develop, gradually taking on a
sharper focus. Most often, the vision will be developed in conjunction
with the management.

Corporate vision and purpose are frequently seen as part of a company's intangible assets. As such, they will be rooted in the company
culture, the organisational structure, the profiles and conduct of the
employees, and the firm's market reputation. Watching over and
conducting a critical appraisal of the corporate vision and purpose,
re-orienting them and anchoring them in the organisation are important tasks for the board of directors, especially as from this starting

point other essential elements, such as management and strategy, can then be addressed.

Although the corporate vision is rarely to be found as an item on the meeting agenda, the board of directors must nevertheless be imbued with that vision. This implies that for example when replacing a director whose mandate has expired or trying to attract new directors, the board will make use of the corporate vision to draw up a profile of the person(s) they are seeking and will make sure that the newcomers are fully aware of the vision.

It's clear that the shareholders will also play a part in establishing the corporate vision, more so at unlisted companies than at stock exchange-listed firms. At listed companies, especially if there's no reference shareholder or significant shareholder, the shareholders will tend to take the corporate vision as a given, with which they're able to align their investment strategy. At family businesses and also enterprises controlled by professional investors, such as investment companies or private equity houses, the shareholders will play a part in establishing, adjusting and keeping a watch over the corporate vision and purpose.

CSR AND SHARED VALUE

Nowadays, you cannot formulate and implement a corporate vision and purpose for a company without drawing up a corporate social responsibility (CSR) plan. You need to work out how the company is going to help improve the society within which it operates and also what it can do to ensure that its activities cause no damage to people, the environment, the climate and society as a whole.

Under the influence of management gurus such as Michael E. Porter, the term corporate social responsibility has now been broadened to embrace a concept known as 'shared value': how can the company, in its interactions with customers, employees and local residents – in short, the community of which it is a part – create a win-win result for everyone? How can employees obtain better training during their working hours? How can the firm deliver good, safe products that both meet customers' needs and at the same time take into account the demands of the environment?

This kind of win-win thinking, which is a radical departure from the "let's get the best returns for the company without bothering too much about our customers, employees, suppliers or the wider society" attitude, is of course first and foremost the responsibility of the CEO and the management. They're the ones who know most about the social challenges the company is facing and the available options. The task of the governing body is to ensure that the subject of CSR and corporate conduct in society is brought to the boardroom table for discussion, that the company's executive management are fully aware of the issues, and that the initiatives they take are properly followed up. CSR is about more than just holding an occasional exhibition or concert, running a 'Let's fight cancer together' campaign or sponsoring a sports team. It's a collection of actions that will do something to identify society's most pressing problems and then bring forward solutions, either alone or in conjunction with partners.

Appointing the right management

In my opinion, the single most important task – and the most difficult task – of a governing body is to ensure that the company or organisation has a top management team in place that matches its corporate vision and purpose. The recruitment of senior managers is of course not a regular agenda item but it is nevertheless important for the board of directors to regularly appraise the management and assess whether the current executive team is still the right match for the corporate vision and purpose and is capable of achieving the desired results.

Replacing senior managers is no easy task and it requires good sense, planning, consensus-building, and also a feeling for the human side. When passing judgement on a person's work and performance, there are quite a number of factors involved. A company's results are in themselves usually quite easy to measure. It's much harder to identify the factors at play and weigh up their impact on the company results. As a number of factors together determine the results, it's not at all easy to assess the importance of each individual factor.

Once again, we may take as an example the Belgian firm Barco, which saw its profits shrinking in the early 2000s. At that time, the euro exchange rate was rising against the dollar, reducing the competitiveness of European companies on non-European markets. At that same moment, Barco was just introducing new products. So, was the slump in profits attributable to the currency exchange rate, the cost factor – which was itself of course partly determined by the euro situation – the fact that the new products were not proving successful, or because the company had chosen the wrong markets for those products? Management does after all have considerable influence over some of those factors.

GOOD SENSE

The stock market is quick to infer that the management is at fault in such cases but, in reality, things are not quite as simple as that. Sometimes directors have to defend the chief executive and the management team against frivolous remarks by analysts. Executives who are seriously trying to manage the company properly deserve to receive the backing of the shareholders. Of course, you can't persist in defending management like this forever, especially if the company's strategy and results are heading in the wrong direction. Sometimes it's not the results that seal the CEO's fate but the fact that friction within the management or the organisation call into question the quality of his or her leadership and finally lead to his or her

> When it comes to assessing a CEO, directors need to get over simple black-and-white thinking.

departure. Quite a lot of these areas of assessment are not simply black and white. Consequently, any decision to ask the CEO to step down will require a lot of good sense from the directors in general and from the board chair in particular.

Whenever chief executives come and go within a short space of time at a company, it's very doubtful that the directors are showing much good sense, whether we're talking about the hiring or the firing aspect. When I talk about good sense, I don't mean that directors should hesitate or keep putting off the dismissal of the CEO; this approach is often the worst possible option. The managers reporting to the CEO usually know pretty well whether s/he is succeeding in hitting the targets and achieving the right results. It's rather like a sports team: very often the players are the first to spot that their trainer is no longer capable of bringing success to the team. A number of times I've had the experience that, following the dismissal of a chief executive, several of the senior managers have come to me as board chairman and asked why it had taken so long to fire the CEO, often adding: *"Surely everybody knew that that CEO no longer had any right to be here?"*

A CEO might in fact actually be relieved to be asked to step down. CEOS are generally sensible people who are well aware of their own limitations and can see for themselves that although they've given their best, their best just wasn't good enough. So why don't they simply resign? For all kinds of reasons, perhaps mainly financial considerations, but one reason may certainly be that it takes a while for the hard truth to sink in that this person is not going to be able to turn the company's fortunes around.

PLANNING

The dismissal of a CEO or senior manager requires both good sense and planning. After all, who exactly is going to replace this top executive? Will the governing body choose a temporary replacement while a thorough search is conducted within or outside the organisation, or should the board immediately appoint a permanent successor to the departing executive? If so, will this be an internal replacement or will you look outside the company? This second option will undoubtedly require much more time, unless of course the company's succession planning is so far advanced that the board already have their eye on a replacement.

Sometimes the board will look within its own ranks for a successor. Studies have in fact shown that this isn't a bad solution, because a sitting director will already be familiar with the company and the issues it faces. Such analyses as have been made indicate that the immediate replacement of a chief executive officer by a board member tends to be more successful than bringing in a new CEO from outside the company, because the new appointee will take longer to work him/herself into the job and there's no guarantee that s/he will be able to find the right rapport with the company. Succession planning that gets underway long before the CEO is fired can be very useful, but then you have to be very cautious. You should probably think carefully about whether the forced departure of the CEO doesn't in fact undermine the planned succession as well. Moreover, whenever a decision is taken to replace a departing CEO with a director, you must take care to ensure that this doesn't lead to a battle between board members who aspire to the job of chief executive.

CONSENSUS

Good sense and planning are indispensable when it comes to replacing a CEO, but it's equally important to forge a strong consensus within the board. This will certainly be necessary if the various directors don't take the same view regarding the supposed failings of the CEO.

Some board members will give more weight to unfavourable market conditions, while other directors will mainly point to the strategic mistakes which they believe the CEO and management have made. Board members may also differ over the amount of time they're

It's essential that
the directors should be
unanimous in their
support for the decision
to replace the CEO.

willing to grant the CEO to get the company back on track. It's therefore very important that the chair of the governing body should try to achieve a broad consensus among the directors. Consensus will also be necessary to prevent divisions breaking out in the board, once the CEO has actually departed, between directors who wanted to carry on with the same chief executive and those who were not of the same mind. The departing CEO might also make use of the differences of opinion on the board to contest the decision or try to squeeze a better severance package out of the firm. It's therefore essential that the directors should be more or less unanimous – or preferably entirely unanimous – in their support for the decision to replace the chief executive.

THE HUMAN SIDE

The dismissal of a CEO can be a personal tragedy for the departing executive. His or her colleagues on the management committee, and the staff reporting to or working directly with the chief executive may also feel the departure acutely. It's therefore very important to ensure that the process is conducted in the right way, with appropriate support provided and due respect shown. I agree that external professional support can be of great help but I do believe that the directors themselves have a large role to play here. However difficult to achieve it might seem, the best outcome is that all concerned become convinced that the departure of the CEO is a good thing for him/her and good for the company. However, following the departure, the board members shouldn't just drop the former chief executive like a stone but try to keep communication channels open. Banishing a person to the wilderness never did anyone any good. This open communication must of course be conducted in a natural way and should be two-sided, so that if the departing CEO doesn't want to have anything more to do with the company, that decision must be respected.

CONTEXT

Everything I've written above about the departure of a chief executive officer depends of course to a very large extent on the context within which the governing body is working. The shareholder structure will strongly influence the kind of discussion that takes place about the dismissal of the CEO or other top managers. A dominant shareholder will certainly wish to be closely involved in any such decisions and might even be the one who starts the ball rolling. If the governing body is working effectively, the dominant shareholder will certainly involve the directors in the process of replacing the CEO. However, sometimes the replacement process goes ahead without the board members being consulted at all. This is often the case when the state is the dominant shareholder. The government sometimes fires a CEO 'off its own bat', leaving the board to sort out all the administrative details of the dismissal afterwards. This is certainly not an example of good governance. For political reasons, the Belgian government for instance tends to cut a few corners in this area.

A particularly delicate problem arises if the CEO under scrutiny happens to be a member of the family that controls the company or if s/he's a shareholder. In such cases the directors will need to approach the situation with a great deal of care and discretion. Nonetheless, if the problems with the top management are serious enough and it would be wise to replace the chief executive, then that should be done. This is also the case where the founders of an enterprise don't subsequently seem capable of running a more complex organisation.

At listed companies, reactions from the stock market have a great influence on any perceived need to make changes at the top. Investors will of course have an opinion about whether or not to replace the management and the directors will have to take their views into account, but they must also try to avoid letting external investors lead them by the nose. If the share price falls, that's not necessarily the management's fault. In such circumstances as these, calls to replace the management are probably the consequence of short-term interests more than anything else.

THE SEARCH FOR A NEW CEO

If the chief executive leaves the company – whether s/he has been dismissed, resigned voluntarily or has reached the age limit for the post – the governing body will have to look for a successor. The options for conducting a search are legion – internal or external recruitment, with or without the aid of an executive search specialist, or based on prior succession planning.

Usually, the board will set up a search committee composed of people from its own ranks. This might be the remuneration committee but it doesn't necessarily have to be. Usually the process begins with the drawing up of a candidate profile, which will be based on the corporate vision and purpose. Is the company planning to achieve growth in the national or international markets? Does the firm need to undergo a radical transformation or not? Is the business facing digital disruption? These are the starting points that you will need to incorporate, in one way or another, into the profile of the new top manager, which will then serve as a guideline for the executive search.

A specialist executive search firm can be commissioned to carry out the search, or else the search committee might prefer to conduct the process itself. In either case, I've always thought that the search should remain focused and discreet. I don't think anyone's best interest is served by throwing the entire process open to the public, as – unfortunately enough – tends to happen at state-run companies. It has never been clear to me what the advantages of that approach are supposed to be.

A major problem with an executive search process, especially if it has to be conducted internationally because the company is aiming for international growth, is the time it will take to appoint a new CEO. This is certainly a point to consider when preparing to dismiss the existing CEO. On the other hand, it's very unpleasant and not very ethical to begin the search process for a new chief executive while the existing CEO is still in the job and knows nothing about his/her imminent departure. It is in any case very naive to imagine that the outgoing CEO won't get to know that you're looking for a replacement for him/her and if that does happen the directors will find their reputations somewhat tarnished.

It's not unusual that only certain board members will be involved in the search for a new chief executive. However, care must be taken to ensure that, once the process is over, all the directors are allowed to express their verdict on the matter, following a face-to-face discussion with the leading candidate, especially if they haven't met him/her previously.

Once again, the context within which the governing body is working will obviously have quite some influence on the process of searching for a new chief executive, and here again the shareholder structure is of great importance. At a company with a dominant shareholder, it goes without saying that this shareholder will certainly be closely involved in the search and will need to approve the outcome. It will be more complicated if we're talking about a family shareholder, in which case it will have to be clarified in the first place whether or not the new CEO is going to be a member of the family. If that is so, then you need to set up a process to ensure that a wise choice can be made between candidates from the family. This will be a highly delicate process but it can turn out well if the directors and shareholders think things through carefully, cooperate well and show respect for each other's roles in the process.

At state-run companies, in Belgium at least, it's often difficult for the governing body to play a meaningful part in the appointment of a new CEO because the Belgian government insists on claiming that

The government's insistence on appointing a new CEO itself is misguided and inappropriate. role for itself. This approach is misguided and inappropriate. It's misguided because the government ought to learn to work with the board of directors that they have appointed. And it's inappropriate because it's always hard for a governing body to exert influence over the executive management if the directors haven't been allowed to play any part whatsoever in the appointment of the chief executive.

Appraisal and remuneration of the CEO, management and directors

In principle, it's the CEO who sets the fixed and variable compensation paid to the management. The managers work under the orders of the chief executive, so it's logical that s/he makes the proposals regarding their salaries and bonuses. Nonetheless, it's customary and also advisable that the compensation to be paid to the members of the management or executive team should have to be examined and approved, first by the remuneration committee and then by the full board of directors. This helps to make the process objective and provides directors with both information on the level of remuneration and also insights into the CEO's assessment of the performance of management personnel. The bonuses granted to the management also set the lower limit for the CEO's bonus. It's logical that when the bonuses paid to executives rise or fall, this movement serves as a guide to what the CEO can expect to receive.

The CEO's salary, bonus, any options granted, plus pension and other benefits allocated are decided by the board of directors. The board will, depending on the context within which it is working (see Chapter 2) take a decision on the basis of a proposal from the remuneration committee. The CEO's bonus is decided separately from the bonus paid to management, but if all the other managers receive a reduced (or no) bonus, it will usually be difficult to grant a higher bonus to the chief executive.

Discussions on remuneration and bonuses are rarely easy. Moreover, it's my impression that in recent years, less use has been made of purely mathematical formulae to determine bonuses. At the start of every year, a number of objectives and targets will of course be set but these are not always expressed in hard figures. The process has become much more discretionary: the results, growth and current value of the company will certainly be taken into account but a range of other factors will be considered as well. The chair usually plays an important role here as it's not easy for a CEO to negotiate with the entire board. Naturally, the fact that the governing body is responsible for deciding on executive compensation strengthens its position. At state-owned companies in Belgium, however, the government likes to make the decisions about top management compensation, often without having any real in-depth understanding of what the CEO has actually achieved over the period. This undoubtedly undermines the position of the board of directors to some degree.

> Conducting an appraisal is about more than just running through a list of targets and seeing whether they've all been met.

Remuneration and performance appraisal should go hand-in-hand. It makes absolutely no sense to decide on the chief executive's annual compensation without holding a discussion about the performance of the CEO and management during the past year. Conducting an appraisal is about more than just running through a list of targets that were set and seeing whether they've all been met. It ought rather to be an overall assessment of performance. Has the CEO succeeded in providing the company with the right leadership so as to achieve the strategy and carry through any necessary transformation of the organisation? Has the management also succeeded in assuring the future of the company?

The compensation received by the CEO and the management are published in the company's annual report. This gives shareholders the opportunity to question the board on the subject. Personally, however, I've received very few comments from shareholders about the remuneration paid to the chief executive officer or the other executives, although there have of course been examples reported in the press of cases where company shareholders have rejected top management compensation packages. That has usually been in a situation where the compensation allocated did not reflect company performance. It's hardly surprising that the shareholders would be unhappy if the company is performing badly and the management bonuses are set at an inappropriate level. They feel the pain of a falling share price and want the management to share their pain. However, with very few exceptions, directors have learned to adjust executive bonuses whenever the company performance leaves something to be desired.

In fact, most of the comments made about the size of management bonuses come from the general public. In Europe, however, and certainly in Belgium, one could hardly say that executive bonuses have got out of hand, especially in comparison with the United States. If the size of the bonuses is in line with rising profits, then it's hard to understand some of the public criticism. If people say that management bonuses shouldn't be paid when a firm is doing well, on the grounds that "*nobody's worth that sort of money*" or that it perpetuates inequalities vis-à-vis the workforce, then we are entitled to ask what will be done with the money that was earmarked for bonus payments. This money won't be divided among the non-management employees because they will already have received their variable compensation package. It will therefore be added to the company profits, so it will be the shareholders who benefit from a decision not to pay bonuses. It still amazes me that there's so much opposition to executive bonuses among the general public. This might not be the case if people knew that not paying management bonuses benefits only the shareholders. Isn't it fairer that those who have actually worked to achieve the results – the CEO, the management and staff – are able to pocket a little bit of the profit that has been made?

As a consequence of making chief executives' remuneration figures public, CEOS have become rather more cautious, sometimes even forgoing a salary raise or a bonus in order to avoid coming under too much scrutiny. If you apply the reasoning I outlined above, you may reach the cynical conclusion that all this is a remarkably good thing for shareholders.

Company directors are also called upon to talk about their own emoluments. These are also made public, at least at stock exchange-listed firms. The way it works is that it's always up to the shareholders to determine the total sum to be paid out to the members of the board. So it's not the directors themselves who decide how large a slice of the cake they'll take, but the shareholders who are providing the funds to do so. And rightly so. The board members then divide the total sum provided between themselves, usually on an equal-shares basis, although the members of the various board committees will normally receive extra compensation for this work, as also will the board chair. It does happen, however, that the chairperson sometimes doesn't receive any extra emoluments, for instance if s/he's one of the shareholders. The emoluments received by directors of listed companies are declared individually, so that anyone and everyone can form an opinion about the level of compensation they receive. Unfortunately, the emoluments received by the directors of not-for-profit organisations are rarely made public, so we shouldn't be surprised that abuses sometimes occur at such organisations.

Approving company strategy

I've always been convinced that the board of directors shouldn't formulate company strategy. I have two reasons for saying this. The first is that the board is not well equipped to formulate a strategy, even if the directors hire in a specialist consultant to assist them. They don't have detailed knowledge of the markets, customers, competitors and technologies that the management either possesses or can obtain. A second reason for leaving the task of formulating company strategy to the CEO and the management is that they're the ones who will have to implement it. Separating the formulation of strategy from

Directors shouldn't be
tempted to take on the role
of strategists themselves.
its execution is not conducive to motivating
managers to get working on it. Moreover, the
management were appointed with a brief
to apply an appropriate strategy in order to
achieve the corporate vision and purpose. Within the framework of
the company's vision and purpose, the CEO and the management
ought to be best placed to work out a suitable strategy. If this is not
the case, then the board has made the wrong choice of managers and
the directors should correct that before they're tempted to take on the
role of strategists themselves.

The directors should however be called upon to approve the strategy drawn up by management. This is one of their fundamental tasks
so they should discuss and vet the proposed strategy with great care,
paying close attention to the potential value-creation – which is, after
all, supposed to be the outcome of the strategy – and also ensuring
that it will be financeable. I have the impression that the requisite
attention is not given often enough to the value creation aspect.

In fact, when assessing any given strategy, the question of whether
the proposed strategy is going to create value for the company and the
shareholders is indeed a difficult point. In principle, it shouldn't be
too hard to calculate the value of a new, or re-designed, strategy. All
you have to do is offset the incoming cash flows from the margins
achieved by entering new markets, introducing new products or
rationalising operations against the outgoing cash flows relating to
the cost of transformation, investment and changes to the working
capital, and then discount the net cash flow using an appropriate
cost of capital.[12]

If this looks quite easy on paper, it's a lot more difficult to do in
reality. First of all, the figures that you need to make these analyses can
be very unreliable – not just because they're based on future market

---

12 Readers who are not familiar with the techniques of net cash flow and
discounted cash flow calculation are advised to consult a corporate finance
manual.

movements, changes to the clientele, and fluctuating margins, but first and foremost because you have to bear your competitors in mind. How are they going to react when you bring your new products to market? Will they start a price war? Or launch new products of their own? Such uncertainties make it hard to judge the level of value creation you can expect the new strategy to achieve and this is something which the directors will have to discuss with management. At least during this discussion you'll be able to focus on concrete issues such as the amount of revenue the company will be able to achieve, the margins it can count on and how to gauge competitors' reactions.

This kind of hard business discussion has the advantage that it tends to create a counterweight to a predominantly technological or overly sales-oriented approach to strategy. All too often, discussions about new technology and sales opportunities take on a highly 'deterministic' tone, creating the impression that there's no real alternative to the proposed strategy. A lot of companies have got into trouble for this very reason and it's here that the governing body has a genuine role to play by insisting on a critical assessment of the company strategy and any necessary adjustments. The board can probably provide more useful input in this area than by trying to assess technologies or grasp the thrusts and counterthrusts of competition – fields in which the chief executive and management are sure to have more up-to-the-minute knowledge than the directors.

An integral part of the strategy discussion is of course the company's financing. Here again, the governing body has a part to play in ensuring that the CEO and the management keep their feet on the ground. Usually the directors are well-placed to keep an eye on the company's debt level, although there are some notorious examples of companies where the board, seduced by the siren song of the supposedly higher profitability that will go hand-in-hand with the level of debt, were prepared to take great risks in order to implement a highly daring strategy.

Approving the budget

There are three basic reasons why the governing body discusses and approves the organisation's budget for the coming year. The budget contains a list of items where revenue, expenses, margins, results and the internal and external financial resources are either stated or estimated. The budget first and foremost enables board members to judge whether the agreed strategy is being properly implemented and how far the organisation has already gone with the implementation. By examining the proposed budget on the table, the directors can also begin to form a view of how successful the agreed strategy is proving to be. They can then subsequently work out whether the organisation has, or is likely to have, the necessary resources to carry out its plans. The budget provides the directors with a forward view of the company's progress over the coming year, allowing them to gauge whether any operational or strategic adjustments will be needed. Last but not least, the budget is a useful instrument for exercising supervision over the CEO and the management.

THE BUDGET AS AN INSTRUMENT OF SUPERVISION

When using the budget as an instrument of supervision, it's advisable to differentiate between three sets of figures: figures from the previous period, the budgeted figures, and the latest actual figures. I always think that it's useful to make two distinct comparisons in relation to the previous and current figures. If the current figures are better than the previous ones, this means that the management has succeeded in achieving a better performance than in the foregoing period. This might be due to a successful strategy, better operational execution, lower costs for the parts or raw materials required to manufacture the company's products, or fortunate circumstances in the markets in which the company does business.

More revealing however when assessing management performance is to compare the latest actual figures with the budget for that period. If the improved figures are still not as high as what was budgeted, this means that the management was too self-confident or too optimistic. They thought they would be able to do more with the company than in fact proved to be the case. Of course, it's quite possible that they suffered some kind of setback or encountered unforeseen headwinds in the marketplace. So it's very useful to see whether the actual figures for new products or services are much lower than the budget projections. If they are, this calls for some vigilance on the part of the directors, because the gap suggests that the chief executive and the management team misjudged the timing and potential success of the market launch of the new products. The same goes for the cost side. If the costs turned out much higher than budgeted, this means that the CEO and management didn't succeed in achieving the planned efficiency improvements.

Another important conclusion can be drawn if the latest actual figures are down on the previous period but this worsening situation was already forecast in the budget. On the one hand, this situation is not very reassuring but at least it shows that the management is capable of correctly anticipating future developments and adjusting the budget in line with their forecasts. This equips them to take the necessary measures in good times so as to safeguard the company against fluctuations in the market.

So how detailed should the budget be before it's tabled for discussion by the governing body? I've observed some wide variations in practice. At some companies, management will provide a lot of detail on each of the various budget items and consequently the budget document turns into a bulky file that threatens to become unclear and unmanageable for

Bulky budget files make it too easy to mask bad news.

the board members. Managers sometimes use such packed-out documents as a way of 'burying' bad news. Afterwards, they can always claim that they had duly informed the board: that the unfavourable information was there in the documents but that the directors had simply overlooked it. This shows a lack of trust between management and the board of directors. I therefore think it's better not to produce too detailed a budget for the board but to draw it up in such a way that the directors are able to form a clear impression of how the company's strategy and business model are working out. The same goes for the resources used to finance the enterprise. If there's any important information in the budget that the board members are not able to extract for themselves, the management should draw their attention to it, even if it's of a negative nature. This approach shows that relations between directors and management are based on thorough mutual trust.

It can also be important for legal reasons for the management to obtain the approval of the governing body for the annual budget. This formal approval empowers the management to go ahead with the planned expenditure. Should any dispute subsequently arise, this will provide the management with legal cover for their actions.

'TARGET-SETTING' VERSUS 'PREDICTIVE' BUDGETING

One budgeting process may differ from another. When the budget for a particular division or department presupposes a particular level of turnover, price level or margin, the management of that department will be expected to achieve the budgeted figure. This is known as target-based budgeting or 'normative' budgeting. If the managers concerned fail to hit the budgeted figures, this may well affect the variable component of their compensation package or even have consequences for their careers. At a not-for-profit enterprise such as a hospital or festival organiser, the budget is usually not strictly target-based but rather a 'predictive' budget or forecast. The chief executive and the management use the budget process in order to draw up a forecast of how the year will turn out. It will set out the total amount of subsidies that will be available, the commercial revenues that are likely to be brought in, and consequently the level of expenditure the hospital or festival organiser will be able to bear during the year. There will still be quite some pressure to achieve the budgeted figures but the target-setting element will, in my experience, be less compelling.

A predictive budget is more like a set of guidelines indicating to the staff what will be possible on the expenses front over the coming year. This type of budget will therefore often be adjusted a couple of times during the year. As new information about income and expenses becomes available, the forecast budget will be adapted accordingly so that everyone can see how things are going. In such cases the budget is more of a forecast than a real budget. A target-based budget may also be adjusted occasionally, but far less often.

A forecast is often also appended to a target-based budget because of course company staff and board members want to know what the year's outcome will depend upon. This is also important for the shareholders and other parties investing in a listed company. They want to know whether the company's expectations and the announcements previously made are likely to become reality. If this isn't the case, the directors will need to approve an alert to warn investors that the results may be disappointing. However, this warning will come on the basis of the forecast, not on the basis of the budget, which remains target-based.

Approving capital investments, acquisitions and mergers

The governing body will also be called upon to approve proposals for capital investments and acquisitions. Going into a merger is an entirely different matter, which I won't discuss here because it's the shareholders who will have to decide on any merger proposals after considering the advice provided by the board of directors and the management.

CAPITAL INVESTMENTS

It's essential that the governing body should be asked to approve any large investments in fixed assets because this kind of item usually exceeds the powers delegated to the management. This is an opportunity for the board to examine whether this capital investment fits with the approved company strategy and can be financed with an acceptable risk profile. Once again here the context within which the board of directors is working is an important factor (see Chapter 2). If the company has a dominant shareholder, then it's quite usual for the board to talk it through with this shareholder, especially if it's a sizeable investment. This is clearly important if, in order to finance the investment, the company will need to find extra funds, which might well raise its level of indebtedness. If we're talking about raising fresh share capital, then it goes without saying that this move will require shareholder approval.

At family businesses, any decision to raise risk capital from third parties will be of great consequence for the family. Not least, it will have an impact on the composition of the governing body as the new shareholders will generally demand representation on the board of directors, which will in turn have consequences for the way the board works.

ACQUISITIONS

The chief executive and the management will also need to obtain the approval of the board of directors for any major acquisitions the company is planning to make. From experience, I've learned to look out for a number of aspects. First of all, does the proposed takeover fit with the company strategy? In most cases, the target company will not make a perfect fit with the strategy, but that need not be an obstacle. Perhaps several divisions of the new acquisition can be sold off. If, however, the company in question would make only a minimal fit with current strategy, then the board should be asking whether it really makes sense to go ahead with the takeover. Nevertheless, the proposed acquisition may provide a useful opportunity to take a critical look at the current strategy.

It's also very important that the directors question the management as to how they intend to integrate and manage the new acquisition. Managers are often rather over-confident about this and think they can just take it all in their stride but experience shows that it can turn out quite differently. The supposed synergies that will be gained should also be explicitly discussed.

Ideally, a clear schedule should be drawn up for the implementation of synergies so that the board can subsequently verify whether the expected synergies are actually being achieved according to schedule. It's also important to examine the proportion of synergies expected to come from growth in turnover and the proportion earmarked from cost savings. The second category is much easier to achieve because such savings usually come under the direct control of the management, whereas turnover-derived synergies can only be achieved if the customers can see the benefits of the new situation. So such synergies are much less certain and will require more time, which will of course affect the profitability of the takeover. Another consideration is how the takeover will affect the company's geographical footprint.

A technology company, which will need to make a number of acquisitions in order to expand its technological capabilities, must guard against taking on too many sites spread across too many different locations with different legislation, employment regulations and social security systems. This may sharply increase the complexity of the organisation and may, in extreme cases, make considerable demands on the managers' skills. For instance, the Human Resources manager of a company that makes acquisitions will see his/

> An acquisition can sharply increase the complexity of an organisation and may in extreme cases make considerable demands on the managers' skills. These are sensitive issues for the directors and the management to deal with.

her job suddenly become much more complicated. Board members will be able to bring to the table a different point of view than the management, who tend to downplay the difficulties associated with this kind of scale changes.

ACQUISITION PRICE

Lastly, there will of course be a boardroom discussion about the acquisition price and the financing of the takeover. I've already addressed this point in Chapter 2 but it's worth pointing out again here that the management will tend to focus their attention on the strategic aspects of the takeover. There's nothing wrong with that. However, it then falls to the board members to correct the sight lines and ask whether the takeover doesn't come at too high a price and, of course, whether it can be financed in a normal manner. This can arouse some friction between directors and management but that's perfectly healthy and it's a necessary part of the process. Perhaps the management will accuse the board of short-sightedness and a lack of strategic vision but that need not be a problem. The number of unsuccessful company acquisitions and the number of enterprises that have 'gone under' because they didn't think through a takeover bid thoroughly enough provide sufficient arguments for the governing body to hold a proper discussion on any proposed takeover.

Making proposals for dividend policy, share buybacks, capital reductions and refinancing

One of the governing body's important tasks is to ensure that the company or organisation has the means to implement its strategy and achieve its vision and purpose. This means that company directors must think about how much risk-bearing capital and debt the enterprise needs in order to finance its assets and activities. If the company has taken in too much risk capital, it will be harder to obtain a decent return on the capital. However, if the firm has too little risk capital and is financing a high proportion of its assets through debt, then it will be running a higher risk.

The board must therefore have a good understanding of shareholder expectations as regards profitability and risk. What trade-offs between risk and return are the shareholders willing to accept? What trade-offs can the company in fact make? The fact is that any trade-off is determined by the relationship between the risk capital and the outstanding debt. This relationship is known variously as the debt ratio, the solvency ratio or the leverage ratio. If the debt ratio is low, then – all else being equal – the profitability of the business will also be low, but so will the risk. If the debt ratio is high, then under unchanged market conditions, the firm's profitability may be high or very high, but the risk will also be high.

The board, which is accountable for the company's profitability and risk profile, has a number of tools to hand in order to exert influence over the debt ratio. Accordingly, the directors will need to make proposals to the shareholders regarding the firm's dividend policy, perhaps for a share buy-back programme, a capital reduction operation or a capital increase through the issuance of new shares. A capital reduction will have to be matched by taking on extra debt. Decisions of this kind will all need to be taken by the shareholders, but the decisions they make will be formulated and put before them by the board of directors for their approval.

Of course, the board members don't formulate those proposals all by themselves. They'll be worked out by management, though perhaps under the guidance of the directors. As with so many other items up for discussion by the governing body, the context makes a very big difference. The most important factor here is the shareholder structure. At some family-owned companies, dividend payments are subordinated to the drive for growth. Family shareholders may prefer to retain as high a proportion of the firm's resources as possible in the business, so as to foster growth or perhaps ensure the company's independence vis-à-vis external financiers. At other family firms however, where a number of branches of the family are represented among the shareholders, they expect the board to make sure a predictable level of dividend is paid out every year. This is likely to have consequences for the company's growth prospects and risk profile. In such cases, the company may have to finance its growth plans by taking on a higher debt ratio, which in turn creates a higher risk profile.

The dividend policy will therefore certainly be influenced by the shareholder structure, but it can also work the other way round. A stock exchange-listed company that opts for a strict, highly predictable dividend distribution policy will attract a particular type of shareholder. Investors who like to see a stable share price and predictable dividend payments will tend to go for the equity of this kind of firm. A good example of this is Gimv, a Flanders-based investment company that opted in the first decade of the 21st century for a predictable dividend policy whereby the dividend would rise slightly every year. This policy encouraged a large number of small investors and pension funds to become shareholders in the firm. A company that adopts the opposite policy – paying a low, rather variable, dividend – will have to try to increase its market capitalisation (stock exchange value) if it wishes to impress investors.

> Companies that decide to pay a low dividend will need to attract investors by increasing their market capitalisation.

Whenever a company has surplus resources, the chief executive and the board of directors will soon come under pressure from the shareholders to repurchase a number of issued shares. The benefit here for the shareholders is that they receive a cash payment and the stock price should rise, so very few CEOs and board members are able to resist this kind of pressure. An extreme method of arranging a share buy-back is to finance it through borrowings that will increase the company's debt ratio, in turn raising the firm's risk profile. This will usually turn out quite well, provided that the markets in which the company does business are growing or as long as the firm is able to take over other companies so as to rapidly increase the consolidated revenue. If growth doesn't materialise or the takeover plan doesn't work out, the company might well get into serious difficulties with this financing strategy.

One of the tasks of the board should therefore be to shield the CEO from any pressure from the equity market to repurchase shares in an unconsidered manner. Shareholders and analysts often call for a share buy-back but the governing body has a responsibility to examine whether this is a sensible course of action for the company at that moment in time. Share buy-backs are sensible if the company has a permanent excess of resources but are not advisable if the sole purpose of the buy-back is to help shore up the share price and help stem a downward price trend.

Nowadays, financial markets have become extremely complex and company finance is about more than just issuing shares and taking out bank loans. This is another subject in which the governing body must be closely involved: board members must have a thorough grasp of the consequences of modern financing constructions for the company's profitability and risk profile.

Discussing HR policy and employee satisfaction

It's a good idea for the governing body to discuss Human Resources policy once a year. In principle, the chief executive and the HR manager, together with the rest of the management, are responsible for drawing up HR policy. Nevertheless, any governing body that really cares about the company or organisation it serves will take a close interest in the HR policies being pursued, how effective they are and the outcome of those policies. This also provides an opportunity for the directors to ask questions about employee satisfaction, the efforts being made to provide training and promote life-long learning at the company, its ability to attract young talent, its diversity, initiatives being taken to counter bullying or sexual harassment, measures to prevent burnout, and so on.

Drawing up the accounts and the annual report

Belgian company law states that the governing body is responsible for drawing up the firm's annual accounts and the annual report. This is logical, since the board of directors is ultimately accountable for the use made of company resources and the results achieved with those resources. The governing body is specifically required to ensure that the accounts and annual report present a true and fair picture of the state of the company and that facts coming to light after the closing of the accounts which might have a bearing on the state of the company are also reported.

Publishing a set of company accounts and an annual report comprises one of the core duties of the board of directors. It's obvious however that the directors don't in practice draw up the accounts and the report themselves. That's best left to management, who have the information, the expertise and the resources to perform this task. Moreover, an external auditor is commissioned to check the management's figures and verify that all assets, liabilities and future commitments are accurately reflected. Nevertheless, the fact that the directors delegate the actual work of drawing up the accounts and the annual report does not exonerate them from their collective responsibility to ensure the accuracy of this published information. The directors remain accountable until the shareholders have formally voted to grant them discharge for the performance of their duties.

Drawing up the annual accounts is ostensibly a purely administrative task for the board members. However, they need to grasp the fact that conflicts of interest may arise between CEO and management on the one hand and the directors on the other. Such conflicts of interest may have to do with the valuation of assets, provisions to be made against potential risks, and even producing an accurate calculation of the company's revenue.

Asset valuations may prove to be a thorny point in the event of a takeover. Suppose that a company has made an acquisition during the past year or in the recent past. It will be in the interest of the CEO and the management to show that the takeover was a good idea, but that may not be the case. Perhaps the company really ought to book an asset impairment or value write-down. In such cases, the board of directors, in conjunction with the external auditors, must be in a position to deliver an unbiased opinion.

A similar problem presents itself when making provisions. If the company is likely to be faced with future commitments, or even a lawsuit, which will entail cost outlay, the board must ensure that provisions are made for such eventualities. The external auditors should of course advise them of this necessity.

One particular problem is how to determine the correct revenue figure. Many companies are able to measure their annual revenue quite accurately. Sometimes, however, things are more difficult. Take for example a digital technology or software company which amasses revenue from licensing agreements. If those licensing agreements cover multiple years, it can be rather unclear how much should be attributed to the current year's revenue. This 'revenue recognition' problem, as it is known, arises quite frequently at tech companies, which of course have an interest in showing their shareholders and potential investors that they're growing fast and generating revenue, while in actual fact the revenue relates to several years. The external auditors have an important part to play here but the directors can also play a useful role in mediating any differences of opinion between the management and the external auditors and ensuring that the right action is taken.

Determining the company's risk profile

Ever since the financial crisis that occurred during the first decade of the 21st century, companies have been paying greater attention to the risks they run. Under the new European banking legislation, banks' governing bodies have an explicit duty to specify their bank's risk appetite. This is right and proper and in fact seems perfectly obvious. However, it's much more difficult than it appears.

Let's start with the banks. Nowadays, banks are much better equipped to handle risks than they were before the crisis. The various risks are measured on a daily basis or even more frequently. Each financial institution has set up an entire internal organisation under a chief risk officer (CRO) to determine and monitor risks. In addition, the CRO reports directly to the risk committee and the board of directors, and stands entirely apart from the financing decisions taken by the bank. In most cases the bank has a large body of statistics, data and figures available to enable it to make a thorough analysis.

But one problem still remains. There is still no standardised method of reporting risks. Each bank creates its own idiosyncratic system, which is then examined and supervised by the regulators but this doesn't mean that there's a standardised approach that applies to all banks. Just compare this with the way companies and banks are required to report their results. Standard reporting mechanisms – such as the Belgian GAAP and the IFRS[13] – have been developed for this purpose. The fact that no standardised system exists for risk reporting makes it hard for board members, because they can never be 100% certain that the system in use at the company really covers all risks. This keeps them on the alert as regards the risks the bank is running – which is, of course, the intention.

At other kinds of companies, there are also quite a lot of risks to identify and keep under control. Nuclear power generators, other energy companies and chemicals producers all face major risks and of course the directors at those firms talk about risks at every meeting. However, food companies also face risks, as do hospitals and also universities. The problem is that the risks are different in nature at each different type of company or organisation, and they therefore call for different assessments. Hence the recommendation that the

---

13 GAAP stands for Generally Accepted Accounting Principles; IFRS stands for International Financial Reporting Standards. This dual system of standards may produce discrepancies in the calculations of the results achieved by a given company.

board should task the management or commission external experts to create a model that will plot the risks, attempt to measure them and estimate how high is the probability that a given risk will actually occur. Directors don't always like to discuss risks because this kind of discussion can get too technical and may give an exaggerated picture of the risks the company or organisation faces. Nevertheless, risk management is one of the core duties of a board of directors.

Communicating results and other price-sensitive information

The governing body has responsibility for approving press releases or other forms of communication targeting the company's shareholders or other investors. Sometimes this can be a pure formality and the press release is waved through at top speed. I think it's regrettable when that happens. A thorough discussion among directors and management about how best to communicate company strategy and results can be very illuminating.

The main purpose of announcements made by listed companies is to support and boost the share price. Sometimes they attempt to communicate bad news in such a way that the share price doesn't begin to slide and that investors continue to have confidence in the management. The management will therefore often be strongly tempted to keep projecting a positive picture of the business, even when things are not going quite so well or the market situation is unfavourable.

Even when the market situation is unfavourable, companies keep putting out positive news reports.

I'll give an example of the kind of announcement that is sometimes put out when a company has achieved poor results or is facing headwinds in the market. This example is not a literal cut-and-paste from a real press release but most company directors, equity analysts, business journalists and investors will immediately recognise the style of expression. The introductory paragraph will sound something like this:

> In spite of unfavourable developments in our markets, the
> company has managed – thanks to our customers' high
> appreciation of our products and our dynamic sales drive – to
> limit the fall in revenue to just 2%. Likewise, we have restricted
> the fall in profit margin to 5%.

Anyone who reads this sort of press release will know full well that the company is in trouble and that the management are attempting to show that they're not to blame for the poor results. In my opinion, the board shouldn't approve this kind of announcement. The press, analysts and investors will see right through the smokescreen and the announcement is very likely to rebound negatively on the company's share price. The directors would do much better to ensure that the announcement is as objective and neutral as possible and that the news is published without any frills. This will be good for the firm's credibility in the longer term.

Not all governing bodies take the time and trouble to vet and approve press releases and announcements, but it does make sense for them to do so, as the example I gave above clearly indicates. It's vital that they conduct a critical examination of the press release announcing the results for the latest period. What is not very useful, however, is when board members show up at the quarterly, half-yearly or annual press conference or meetings with analysts. Experience has taught me that when directors give interviews to analysts and journalists it rarely provides any added value and can actually arouse confusion about who is the real boss of the company. The exception here is if the results are so poor that analysts and journalists start to speculate about whether the management is about to be fired or the company about to be sold off. In such cases, it can be useful for board representatives to be present in order to show support for the management and give a signal on behalf of the shareholders that there are no thoughts of selling the

> It usually does very little good when board members make statements at press conferences.

company – provided of course that the board is quite clear on both of these points.

It can however certainly be useful for board members at unlisted companies or firms with a reference shareholder to stay in contact with the shareholders. After all, it's the shareholders who have entrusted the directors with the duties they perform at the company. It also makes sense for the board members to present the latest results in tandem with the management. The governing body at this kind of company tend to be much closer to the shareholders and the directors can provide support to the management in explaining company results and strategy. This also enables the directors to hear, or get a feeling for, the shareholders' reactions and their expectations vis-à-vis the board of directors and the management.

Preparing for AGMs and EGMs

I always think it's important to prepare properly for the annual general meetings (AGMS) of shareholders and extraordinary general meetings (EGMS). As I mentioned in Chapter 2, I think it's right and proper that all shareholders should be well informed about what's happening, even if only a small group of shareholders is going to be present or represented at the meeting.

The preparations begin for the members of the board when they approve the draft agenda, proposals for dividend distribution or other shareholder payments, and proposals to re-appoint board members and/or appoint new directors. These are very important matters. On the agenda will be other items such as granting discharge to the directors for the performance of their duties, the corporate governance report, and the report on directors' emoluments and management compensation packages.

The number of shareholders who wish to put questions to the CEO and board members at the AGM is not always very large but there will usually be some shareholders whose in-depth knowledge of the company enables them to ask searching questions and make sharp digs at the management. A few shareholders will submit questions in advance and it's very important to prepare answers to these questions very carefully. It may be that such questions relate to confidential information, so that a full answer may jeopardise the company's competitive position. In such cases, the law permits the board to decline to give a complete answer. On the other hand, the CEO, management and directors are not entitled to simply refuse to answer all the questions put, or give an empty answer to each question. Company stewards sometimes forget that they're obliged to answer all questions from shareholders, provided that their answers will not damage the company.

The question-and-answer sessions at an AGM can take up quite a lot of time and the chair and chief executive would therefore often prefer to put an end to the session. However, the legal provisions on this subject are quite clear: shareholders have the right to keep asking questions for as long as they wish, provided that they don't simply keep repeating themselves. It's therefore up to the directors and management at companies with highly active shareholders to set off for the meeting well prepared and ready to answer shareholders' questions calmly. In fact, directors can sometimes learn quite a lot from the questions that shareholders raise.

Taking governance-related decisions

Quite a lot of agenda items for meetings of the board of directors have to do with corporate governance. At most companies and organisations, the governing body will decide the contents of the governance charter. This document will set out the governance structure and lay down principles for directors' conduct both inside and outside the organisation. One of the most important structural elements of practical corporate governance is the setting up of committees, including an audit committee, a risk committee, a remuneration committee and a governance committee.

Well-run boards take steps to ensure that their committees don't drift away from the main board. Committees are there to help the directors fulfil their tasks of setting the course for the company and supervising management actions, by providing vital information. They are basically advisory bodies and must not usurp the role of the board. That may sound perfectly clear, but in practice it's rather more difficult. Board members have a tendency to view everything that has been dealt with in one of the committees as decided and believe that the last word on the matter has been spoken. It shouldn't happen like that. Directors who aren't sitting on a particular committee shouldn't take the attitude that the subjects discussed there have nothing to do with them. This is why I'm not in favour of setting up a strategy committee, because board members who aren't appointed to that committee often find themselves virtually squeezed out of the decision-making 'inner circle'. This is bound to lead to tensions and some members of the governing body may simply disengage. Directors must always remain convinced that they occupy a full and valued position on the board and that the committees are there to help them carry out their duties. They must not be made to feel that the committees are depriving them of their responsibilities.

Another governance item is the appraisal of directors. This is no simple matter. Some directors are independent, others are there to represent a particular shareholder. In this situation, it's far from easy to make assessments of individual performance, because then you're essentially assessing how the shareholder came to designate that particular director. This can be especially problematic at family companies. Nor is it easy to make individual assessments of directors appointed by the authorities to sit on the board of companies in which the state holds a stake. This is why I would advocate making an assessment of the performance of the governing body as a whole. I think it's much more useful to ask how the board of directors is performing as a whole than how such and such a director has been performing.

The main reason for paying more attention to the board of directors as a whole than to individual directors is that the governing body works

Directors should not be
pushed into competing with
each other.

as a collective. It's in no-one's interest to assemble a group of high-powered directors if those highly qualified individuals aren't able to work together to direct and supervise the organisation. Nor is it a good idea to create competition between board members as to who is the best director and who is only second-rate. At the end of the day, they need to work together as a single governing body.

The governing body also has the task of proposing new directors and renewing the mandates of sitting directors. A lot of different elements come into play here. If we're talking about a director who'll be representing a particular shareholder, then it will be that shareholder who proposes a candidate. Usually the board chair and the chair of the appointments committee will first be sounded out confidentially to see how the proposal is received. However, this doesn't always happen and proposals are not always accepted. Nevertheless, a board of directors will always be a body in which various interests are represented and the directors don't always have a free hand in choosing who should represent the various interests.

In addition to board members put forward by a major shareholder, a number of independent directors will also be appointed. It is the task of the sitting directors to conduct a search for suitable candidates and propose them to the AGM. One aim will be to complement the capabilities of the existing directors, so a list of skills and talents already available on the board will usually be compiled so as to identify any missing expertise which the governing body might need going forward. This exercise will enable profiles of the new directors to be drawn up.

Those profiles should also take into account the need for diversity – especially gender diversity – in the governing body. In most countries, this is prescribed by law, but the legislation doesn't usually insist on diversity at all companies and organisations. Nevertheless, I think all organisations ought to be looking at how they can achieve gender diversity, whether they have a legal obligation to do so or not.

Any forward-looking company or organisation should take steps to ensure that it has both men and women sitting on its governing body. Gender diversity should of course also be combined with other forms of diversity. For instance, a company that does business internationally will want to appoint some foreign directors. A financial institution will benefit from having some entrepreneurs on its board alongside the finance experts because those businesspeople are likely to have regular contact with a major segment of its clientele.

Diversity is, quite rightly, increasingly seen as having a positive effect on the performance of a governing body, because it can help to encourage more in-depth reflection when making decisions. This positive effect can arise from the fact that greater diversity among board members is bound to ensure that a wider range of experiences, views, standpoints and skills is brought to the table. But things may go wrong. Concentrating too hard on ensuring diversity may mean that there's a lack of specialist knowledge among board members or that such knowledge is unequally distributed among the directors. It's therefore important when onboarding new directors to look for people who will increase overall diversity and at the same time also be capable of grasping the technical aspects of the decisions that have to be taken. Bringing together on the board a number of individuals whose backgrounds are so diverse that they have nothing in common might make it impossible to reach consensus or lead to a situation where only those board members who have the technical expertise to understand the topics that require decisions are really up to the job and all the others slavishly bow to the leadership of the initiated.

A board of directors is not a little social club or a group of people who are so determined to be nice to each other that they could never bring themselves to make a critical comment towards another member. On the contrary, the governing body must be able to hold a free and frank discussion, but at the same time must not turn into a sort of debating society where consensus can never be reached. This is an important point to consider when onboarding new directors. Nobody wants to have a new board colleague who tries to obstruct

| A governing body is not a little social club, but must still be able to reach consensus. | every decision or wants to call his or her lawyer before giving approval to any proposal. Directors who can't get along with each other or with the CEO and the |

company management will not be an asset when it comes to cooperation in the boardroom. Under normal circumstances, this shouldn't prove to be an insurmountable obstacle. However, in times of crisis, when the company needs to act fast, it's undoubtedly a plus to have a board of directors who are able to work well together.

Other agenda items

Most governing bodies discuss far more subjects than just the ones listed above. I'll mention a few of them here.

APPROVING A PROPOSED TAKEOVER BID ON THE COMPANY

If another firm launches a takeover bid on the company, this is usually a matter for the shareholders. If, however, the company has a fragmented shareholder structure, the governing body will have an important role to play. The directors, assisted of course by the CEO and the management, will need to advise the shareholders with regard to the takeover bid. This is no easy task. On the one hand, the natural reaction of the company will probably be to opt to prolong its independent existence; on the other hand, the interests of the shareholders, who might well be able to make a capital gain, must be taken into account. If the company has a highly concentrated shareholder structure, with a reference shareholder, then the board and the management will usually play a very subordinate role in the proceedings. The reference shareholder will expect the management to give a helping hand in examining the bid, but both board and management have a duty to ensure that they continue to serve the interests of all shareholders and the company as a whole. It's quite difficult to achieve this delicate balance. In such cases, it's not unusual for the governing body and the management to seek the advice of investment banks and/or a law firm that specialises in such matters.

The handling of a takeover bid on the company becomes even more complex if the bid is made by the reference shareholder. If the bidder is not able to negotiate the acquisition price directly with the other shareholders, then it will fall to the independent directors on the board to make an assessment of the bid on the table, judging in particular whether the bid price is fair.

It's obvious that this is a very difficult task, from several points of view. First and foremost, in many cases independent director appointments are subject to a vote in the AGM, and while they carry the title of 'independent' director, their appointments will nevertheless usually depend on the vote of the reference shareholder. Consequently, a company needs to have directors who are not just officially 'independent' from a legal standpoint but are genuinely able to act independently in behaviour and spirit.

Another problem is that independent directors cannot always obtain the detailed information necessary to make an independent judgement of the takeover bid price and will probably need to call on legal and financial experts. They will of course have to obtain the money for this from the management. There is in fact something to be said for not forcing all the shareholders to pay for these professional assessments but asking the bidder to bear the cost of the objective analysis commissioned by the independent directors. One last difficulty may be that the management are not entirely unbiased with regard to the bid. The reference shareholder will probably have put out some signals in advance to the incumbent management as to how their future will look if the bid goes through successfully and whether or not they'll be able to stay on at the company after the takeover. All these factors make it especially difficult for independent directors to assess a takeover bid in a way that's fair to minority shareholders.

CUSTOMER SATISFACTION

The governing body is not responsible for customer satisfaction. This is a task for management. It is however the task of the board of directors to ensure that customer satisfaction is measured and the results analysed. The board might even be able to insist that the CEO take the results of customer satisfaction surveys into account when calculating the variable component of employees' remuneration packages.

In general, however, the board of directors must insist that customer satisfaction be measured and that management provide an explanation of the results. In doing so, the board is not usurping the role of management, but simply ensuring that the subject receives the necessary attention. Sometimes directors are directly contacted by customers with a complaint. Occasionally these come from 'professional complainants', but they still deserve a response. In other cases, these will be serious complaints. Not every complainant has the perseverance to take a grievance up to the highest level of the organisation but they might approach a board director simply because they haven't managed to obtain a suitable answer at other levels of the organisation. In such cases, the director should avoid getting directly involved in the complaint. S/he should ask the organisation to investigate the complaint and resolve the matter if that is desirable and feasible. The director should restrict his/her involvement to monitoring the response that the organisation gives to the complainant and informing the CEO of the situation.

APPROVING POLICY DOCUMENTS AND MODIFICATIONS TO THE DOCUMENTS

The governing body draws up basic documents, such as the company statutes and the corporate governance charter, and will also propose changes to the statutes. It then falls to the shareholders to approve these documents. There are other documents that don't really require the approval of the shareholders, although this of course depends on the context in which the governing body is working (see Chapter 2). These documents may have to do with the ethical code governing the conduct of the CEO, the management and also the members of the board. Examples of this are the procedures regarding dealing in the shares of the company and receiving gifts from business contacts. It's a good idea to have all these documents approved by the board so that they take on the force of a sort of internal regulation or law, which will guide the actions of everyone working at the organisation.

APPROVING AND MONITORING MAJOR RESTRUCTURINGS

If the organisation is undergoing a major transformation, where new technologies are being introduced, departments reorganised, and staff laid off or forced to change jobs, then the governing body ought to be asked to approve and monitor the changes. A restructuring process is a complicated exercise for management and for the organisation as a whole, and is often fraught with tension and personal conflict. The backing of the directors for such moves is therefore welcome.

To sum up

In the last few pages, I've shown why a governing body is likely to have a very full agenda. The directors don't necessarily have to reach a formal decision on every item on the agenda, but they should at least be well informed on every subject. Very often, they will need to give their approval and sometimes they will in turn need to obtain the approval of the shareholders.

Once again, it goes without saying that the board agenda will be largely determined by the context in which the board of directors is operating. As I've repeatedly pointed out, the shareholder structure and the fact of being a listed or unlisted company make a very big difference. The governing body of a not-for-profit organisation may have to deal with a wider agenda as the management at such organisations is often less well-trained and will tend to play the role of general secretariat to the board.

In the following chapter, I'll discuss the running of board meetings. After that, we'll take a look at the role of the board chairman or woman, as it's this person who will, in tandem with the chief executive, plan and draw up the agenda over the year. S/he will need to ensure that the relevant documents are available so that the various agenda items can be properly addressed. Moreover, the board chair must ensure that the agenda items are dealt with during the session and that as few items as possible are postponed to the following meeting.

CHAPTER 5

Conduct of board meetings

How to ensure that all opinions are heard

How are meetings of the governing body actually run? How often do the directors meet? When does a meeting start? When is the meeting over? How are the various items discussed? Is there a lot of disunity? How are discussions conducted between the CEO and the rest of the board and between independent and executive directors? Is there usually a relatively open and frank exchange, or are the meetings dominated by a couple of directors? Does the board actually take a vote on decisions? Are there frequent information leaks? In the following pages, I'll try to describe how a board meeting generally goes.

A BOARD MEETING CAN BE CONSIDERED A SUCCESS IF IT PROVES able, within a reasonable time frame and in a goal-oriented manner, to help the governing body to fulfil its duties of setting the course for, and supervising, the organisation, setting standards and taking responsibility for what happens. This will only be possible if the meeting is well-prepared and well-run, and if the decisions taken and approvals given at the meeting are subsequently implemented in a proper manner. In the following sections, I will explain how this can be done.

The meeting documents

A meeting of the board of directors can be said to begin a few days before the official start time. Several days in advance, the company secretary or board secretary will send each of the directors an invitation to attend, together with the meeting agenda, the documentation on each agenda item and a proxy form. These may be sent through the post or by email but it's an increasingly common practice to use only digital channels for distribution of the board 'papers'. This approach is probably good for the environment but is not entirely problem-free. I'll come back to this point later.

Any governing body whose members do not regularly receive in advance of the meetings the documentation on every point due to be discussed will never be able to fulfil its course-setting and supervision duties. Some years ago, it was still customary for no documents to be sent out in advance. Papers used to be handed out during the meeting and then collected back in again afterwards. I can well understand taking this kind of approach in exceptional circumstances such as a highly sensitive merger proposal – where any suspicion of a leak can have very negative consequences for a company and might even lead to its having to pay out damages. In all other cases, however, I think that withholding documents from board members is an insult to the directors and shows a total lack of trust. If board members are to carry out their tasks properly, they need to have access to the supporting documentation. Moreover, the board papers must be made available in good time so that the directors can read, re-read and study them thoroughly. It's a basic principle that a director who intends to carry out his or her duties properly must be allowed to prepare thoroughly for the board meeting, even though some directors may perhaps not take their preparation quite so seriously as others.

As I just mentioned, nowadays there's an increasing tendency to distribute meeting documentation electronically. This is usually done using a specially-designed software program and via special servers, so as to ensure security. This is necessary to prevent hackers from stealing information intended for board members and also to stop recipients forwarding documents to third parties. Of course, hard copies of the documents can also disappear or be passed on to others but this is less easy to do than through digital media.

Not that the documentation contains such a lot of secrets, but you cannot allow information on management appointments, company strategy, business results or mergers and acquisitions to come out at just any moment. With some very important exceptions, board documents lose their confidential status after a couple of months. However, a problem that can arise when working with electronic documents for governing body meetings is that the directors find it harder to annotate the documents with their comments and that any annotations made are not

Documents quickly lose their confidential status if you attach them to an email.

always preserved. When directors step down from the board at the end of their mandate, they ought to continue to have access to all the documents and the annotations they made. Some companies feel that this is quite unnecessary, but they forget that directors remain accountable in the future for the decisions they have approved, and so they must be able to go back and find specific documents annotated with their concerns and comments.

In the days leading up to a board meeting, telephone calls tend to go back and forth among the directors and with the chief executive. Most of the time, this is not about plots, conspiracies or forming blocs. Directors simply tend to seek extra information and like to know what their colleagues think of a given proposal. The CEO may also phone up in order to provide additional information. The chairperson will also often spend some time on the phone ahead of a meeting – usually to gauge the mood of the directors: are there still any questions to answer and what do they think about the proposals on the table?

During the days leading up to the meeting, it will also become clear which of the directors will be able to attend the session in person, who intends to participate by phone link or video conferencing channels and who will arrange for proxy representation. I always think it's a good idea for an absent board member to give his/her proxy to another director in the same category. An independent director should ideally be represented by another independent director. A director who represents a particular shareholder ought to give a proxy vote to a director representing the same shareholder or one with links to that shareholder. It's not uncommon for proxies to be given to the chair but the company statutes often limit the number of proxy votes that can be assigned to any one person. This is right and proper if you wish to prevent abuses. In principle, every member of the board ought to attend its meetings. People may sometimes be unable to do so for very good reasons but this shouldn't happen too often. Any directors who absent themselves regularly will tend to estrange themselves from their colleagues and find that their knowledge of the organisation diminishes.

How detailed should the documents prepared for board meetings be? It's not easy to strike the right balance here. At some organisations – and I have the feeling that this is more often the case at not-for-profit organisations – the management is of the opinion that the documentation can never be detailed enough and consequently thick packets of papers or gigabytes of attachments are sent flying around. Members of the governing body have to know everything, so, of course, they end up knowing nothing, because none of the directors is able to find his or her way through the clutter of information. There are also organisations where the opposite approach prevails: as little information as possible is provided, under the motto: "*Whatever you do, don't frighten the directors.*"

Clearly the right path lies somewhere in the middle of these two extremes. The people drawing up a document for a particular point on the agenda for a board meeting should ask themselves four questions: 1) What issues do we need to inform the directors about? 2) Why are these important issues for the company or organisation? 3) What options are there for solving these issues? 4) What will be the consequences of each of the solutions put forward? Asking this kind of question will turn the relationship between the management and the board members around. Instead of forcing the directors constantly to go searching through the documents, management will inform them about the issues. I think that this approach is more conducive to fruitful cooperation at the top of the organisation and doesn't force board members to play policeman. This doesn't of course stop the directors carrying out their duties and exercising critical judgement. They shouldn't just sit passively waiting for management input.

Creating this new kind of relationship between the governing body and the management requires that specific meeting documentation will be made available to the directors – and that's of course precisely where the shoe pinches. The CEO and the rest of the management don't want their staff to spend a large part of their time drawing up special documents just for meetings of the board of directors. They would much rather provide the directors with internal documents from the executive board, accompanied by a suitable title page. This not only saves time but also helps to ensure that you don't have different documents circulating, perhaps conveying slightly different messages – which is likely to lead to confusion. Nevertheless, I think it makes sense and leads to better decision-making if supporting documents for items to be dealt with during the board session are produced with their own particular style designed to make the points at issue crystal clear for the directors. This is better than forcing them to go searching through a bulky file to see where the problems lie or having to make do with scanty documents that contain only good news.

The meeting

The governing body will come together on a regular basis but it doesn't necessarily have to be every month. A recent survey conducted by US-based executive search and leadership consultancy Spencer Stuart revealed that the governing bodies of Belgian stock exchange-listed companies meet on average about eight times a year. We may suppose that this average figure covers a wide variation. You can certainly find boards that come together more often than that – once a month for instance – just as there are others which gather once per quarter at the most. The frequency of board meetings differs from company to company and organisation to organisation. It will also depend on the organisation's size and scope of activities. In order to fulfil its duties, the governing body must, at the very least, meet to approve the accounts, make proposals for dividend distribution and authorise the invitations to the AGM.

Apart from the face-to-face meetings, sessions are held now and again via telephone link or using video conferencing equipment. This can be highly convenient for approving a given document. However, if an open discussion on an important subject is called for, a remote meeting doesn't allow directors to observe the body language of their board colleagues and the management and to get a feel for just how strongly they support the proposal on the table.

Now that all the board members have received the relevant documents and have been able to prepare themselves, they're ready to attend the meeting. It might perhaps be useful to say a word about the seats which they occupy around the table. There are different customs in use. At some companies or organisations, the seats are allocated in advance and designated using name cards. I can see two reasons for doing so. In one governing body, the directors will always be seated in the same place, while at another, there will be an attempt to ensure maximum rotation. In fact, the only really 'fixed' seats are those of the chair, the CEO and the board secretary. Encouraging board members to switch seats can be of great psychological benefit, a point to which I'll come back in a moment. Fixed seating may lead to a sort of hierarchical attitude, which can often inhibit free and frank discussion.

Board debates

The chair will usually open the board meeting with a discussion of the minutes of the previous meeting. Quite often, the directors will already have had the opportunity to make comments. A good principle to follow is that the minutes must provide a good, but concise, reflection of the discussions that took place at the previous meeting and they must accurately describe the decisions taken. This is quite important because the company can then subsequently use the minutes to prove to third parties what decisions were taken with regard to appointments, takeovers, investments and so on, and that the budget – which empowers the management to spend money – was approved. I think it's important not to turn the approval of the minutes into an empty formality, along the lines of: "*Everyone's in agreement, I take it?*", but to actually go through them page by page and see that everything's in order. This can be done quite quickly and it doesn't have to take up a great deal of time. What you should avoid, however, is repeating over again the discussions from the previous meeting. The minutes are supposed to be a reflection of the previous meeting and the decisions taken. They should not be the starting point for re-opening those previous discussions.

There's an important difference between minutes taken at a board meeting in the United States – at least the board of a venture capital firm in Silicon Valley – and those taken at a Belgian company. In the US, minutes are very formal and contain only the decisions taken, set out in suitably legalistic jargon, while at Belgian firms the minutes tend to be more extensive, although the old custom of making virtually literal transcriptions of the discussions no longer applies in Belgium either. Moreover, during my time in the United States I got the impression that approval of the previous minutes came as the last point on the agenda – almost as a sort of afterthought – while in Belgium this is normally the first item of business. I think that the Belgian approach is better because approving the previous minutes is a good way to start the meeting: first reminding ourselves what we said, approved and decided last time before turning to what we have on the table today.

After approving the minutes of the previous meeting, the board will normally take a look at the to-do list. The purpose of this is to ensure that subjects which were regarded at some moment in the past as important enough to be discussed at a future board meeting don't get forgotten and that management is tasked to do something about those matters.

Following approval of the minutes and the to-do list, the chair will usually hand over to the chief executive officer to go through what has happened at the company since the last meeting. The CEO will also comment on noteworthy events and any press releases put out by the company or the competition. This is also a good opportunity for the directors to put questions to the CEO or the executive directors. Following the chief executive's report, often amplified by comments from other executive directors, the meeting will be ready to deal with the specific topics of the day.

Every item should ideally be introduced by the manager who drew up the document. There are a lot of advantages to this approach but also some disadvantages. One significant advantage is that board members will then hear the point of view of the expert in the matter.

The presenter is also best-placed to answer any questions expertly. Another advantage is that this helps the directors to get to know the management. If you allow a different department manager to present each separate item, then the board will get to know the key members of the wider management team, and at the same time the managers who make the presentations will also get to know the members of the board better and become more familiar with the workings of the governing body, which they would otherwise not have much opportunity to do.

Now a word about the disadvantages. I've discovered that it's not easy to get managers to show time discipline when making their presentations. They often go into too much detail and digress too much. This is understandable. They're specialists in their field and they want to show that. Moreover, they're often tempted to present matters in a needlessly complicated way, hoping to impress the board, but this usually has the opposite effect. A manager who is able to explain in a short and pithy manner what the members of the board need to know and why, and what options there are for solving any problems, will generally score highly with the directors.

> Managers who wish to score highly with the board should keep things short.

Decision-making

Following the presentation of the subject, the discussion begins, with the aim of making a decision, giving approval to a proposal or taking note of the information. This is where the chairperson needs to watch out. Basically, there are two sorts of board member: the talkers and the quieter ones. Both groups are sensible enough people but the talkers have a tendency to dominate the meeting with their opinions and silence the quieter ones too quickly. The decision can therefore very easily come out on their side as not all the opinions around the table are being openly expressed. Therefore, the chair basically needs to ensure that the talkers talk rather less and the quieter ones talk a little bit more. In fact, board chairs have a few tricks at their disposal to prevent meetings being entirely dominated by the talkers.

MEETING TRICKS

The first, quite simple, trick to help run governing body meetings is regularly to change the order in which the directors are called upon to make their contributions to the debate on any agenda item. I've attended board meetings where there was a sort of 'pecking order' for directors' comments, based on seniority and social prestige. The most senior director was asked to speak first, and so on, and the last to speak was always the youngest member of the board. This wasn't such a good idea as regards exchanges of views, because once the most senior director had spoken, most of the others endorsed his opinion, which of course wasn't conducive to an open debate.

A similar situation arises when the representative of an important shareholder or the reference shareholder is sitting on the board of directors. If this person always gets to speak first, it will be difficult for other directors to express a contrary opinion. You can solve this problem to some extent if the chair asks a different board member to make the opening remarks on each agenda item. This forces directors to express their own views and not simply build further on what the senior board member or the representative of a major shareholder has just said.

Another trick is to designate a director in advance as the first contributor to the discussion on an agenda item. This has more than one advantage. There's always someone who's going to express critical observations or doubts and this is likely to inject greater variety into the debate.

A last little trick, though not so elegant, can be put into action as follows: if the board chair knows that a particular director has a negative opinion of the motion, s/he can invite that board member to speak. That will put the recalcitrant director on the spot, but it's an effective means of ensuring that all opinions are aired.

I've underlined here the need to have an open debate, in which all opinions are heard. However, this shouldn't result in a situation where the board doesn't reach a conclusion and come to a final decision on the item in question. An exchange of views among directors might take quite a long time, which is fine, but a governing body mustn't be allowed to turn into a mere talking shop or become an obstacle to the workings of the company or organisation.

THE ROLE OF THE CEO

So what's the role of the CEO in all this? I think that s/he ought to take part in the debates as an ordinary board member. S/he'll be able to come up with counter-arguments to those who would reject the management proposal and put forward extra information that the directors hadn't taken into account, or perhaps call on one of the executive directors to shed some further light on the subject. It is of course important that the CEO shows, through the arguments presented, that s/he strongly supports the proposal(s) on the table. There shouldn't be a situation where the executive board is divided on the subject and the governing body is simply being used as a means of settling differences of opinion among the management.

Board members who don't agree with the chief executive's opinion must of course be free to express their views openly but they shouldn't adopt an offensive tone or start attacking people. The directors should endeavour to convince the CEO with arguments rather than try to push him or her into a corner – which will solve nothing and may create bad relations between CEO and management on the one side and some or all board members on the other. Some degree of tension at the top of an organisation is unavoidable but if it gets out of hand it's likely to end up damaging the company.

If managers sit on the board as executive directors, their presence will influence the way discussions in the boardroom go. Usually, executive directors will back the CEO's opinions. Unless there is some degree of friction, they won't openly contradict the chief executive. This is perfectly normal and the other directors ought to show respect for this stance. Executive directors are of course able to bring extra information and insights to the table but I don't think that having a repetition in front of the independent and other directors of the discussions that have already taken place among the management is the best way to run a meeting.

THE FINAL DECISION

After all arguments have been heard, it's time to make a decision. How do you do that? I think the chair should attempt to summarise the arguments and formulate a decision proposal or adapt the proposal on the table. It's good practice to ensure that the document on which the decision is to be based contains a written proposal for decision so that there's no doubt about what exactly has to be decided. The chair can then confirm to the board members that the written proposal on the table is the proposal to be considered or s/he can suggest modifications to that original proposal, on the basis of the arguments that have been put forward during the meeting. However, if the chairperson does so, s/he must be sure that s/he has the support of the CEO and a large proportion of the board.

Does the proposal have to be put to a formal vote? This might be the case in exceptional circumstances but it's not desirable. It's much better to ask each board member whether s/he is able to back the proposal. It's important to do this so as to avoid a situation where one director subsequently starts yelling that s/he was not in agreement. If no-one voices a wish to vote against or abstain on the proposal, the minutes should state that the proposal was carried unanimously. Of course, the decision that's recorded in the minutes must correspond to what was agreed at the meeting. Sometimes the temptation to slightly deviate from that verbal agreement will arise but this is not a sign of good governance. Such deviations are, moreover, punishable by law. If it should appear that some adjustment(s) to the decision are needed, it's better to have those adjustments explicitly approved at a subsequent board meeting.

During the board meeting, the chairs of the various board committees – including the risk committee, audit committee, remuneration committee and appointments committee – should report back on what they've been discussing. They must also table the committees' decision proposals, as these need to be approved by the full board.

AOB AND CLOSE OF MEETING

Traditionally, before closing the meeting, there will be an agenda item known as Any Other Business (AOB). Under this item, the directors can raise any subject on which they have issues or on which they would like more information. It's important not to treat this agenda point as an expendable item but to give every board member the chance to speak if s/he wishes. The motto should be: There are no stupid questions, only stupid answers.

However, the meeting cannot be said to be over the moment the last word has been spoken. In practical terms, it's not really over until the minutes have been approved at the next board session.

It's increasingly common for companies to hold offsite board meetings – i.e. the governing body will meet at a different location from the normal boardroom. Such sessions also tend to run for longer. Sometimes the board members and management will stay at the venue overnight in order to make sufficient time for their gathering. The offsite approach can also be used to arrange visits to the company's establishments and sites abroad so that directors get to know those foreign operations better.

The main subject on the agenda for such offsite meetings is usually company strategy. The offsite arrangements provide sufficient time for this and the discussion can be held in a more informal style. Members of the executive board or management board will also usually be invited to these special meetings of the governing body. This means that not only will the directors get to know each other and develop a better understanding of each other's points of view, but they'll also get to know the managers who are running the various divisions and departments of the company. This is very important because in future, whenever a discussion arises about replacing managers or planning management succession, the directors will know at first hand who they're talking about.

To sum up

The governing body works exclusively through its meetings. It's therefore extremely important that those sessions are run well. You can't run an effective meeting without good supporting documentation. Secondly, the discussions must be open and frank. A board meeting packed with hidden agendas will never enable the directors to fulfil their duties in a proper manner. However, open and frank discussions must not be allowed to get in the way of the decision-making process. By the close of the meeting, all the knotty problems should have been unravelled and sorted out. It may of course happen that a final decision is carried over until the following meeting but that should not be regular practice. The organisation is expecting the governing body to take the necessary decisions.

In some countries, the meetings culture is such that decisions are often taken 'in the corridor'. This euphemism basically means that things are decided outside the boardroom. The directors are then simply presented with the decisions and asked to rubber-stamp them. This is not good practice because it deprives the operations of the governing body of any real meaning and reduces some directors to a third-class role. While it can certainly be useful to have informal consultations in advance in the corridors so as to be able to understand directors' viewpoints more clearly and provide explanations where necessary, it's much better to hold an open, frank discussion during the board meeting prior to taking a decision.

CHAPTER 6

The role of the chair

More than just presiding the meeting

When, on introducing myself to people, I tell them
that I'm the chairman of a company, they often ask me:
"So what does a chairman actually do?" I'm no longer
surprised when I hear this and I can fully understand
why they ask this question.

Under the influence of management books by US authors, plus the media and financial analysts, all the attention in recent years has been lavished on the role of the chief executive officer. This is perfectly understandable, since the separate role of board chair is almost unknown in American business life. The top manager at a US corporation usually fulfils a double function, with the title of Chairman (or woman) & CEO. Americans have always tended to favour this combined role because of fears that having more than one person at the top of the organisation would result in conflict. And while pressure from the corporate governance movement has led quite recently to some questioning of this concentration of decision-making powers in the hands of a single person, most US firms still today stick to the system of combining the roles of board chair and chief executive.

Things are not quite the same in Europe. The typical approach in the United Kingdom is to strictly separate the roles of chair of the board of directors and managing director (equivalent to chief executive officer). Moreover, the role of non-executive directors has been steadily increasing in recent years. In France, where some large corporations still adhere to the system of combining in the post of Président Directeur-General (PDG) the roles of board chair and chief executive, as in the United States, measures have been taken to limit the powers of the PDG by conferring greater powers on the board of directors as a whole to monitor the executive actions of the PDG and mandating the appointment of a majority of non-executive directors on the board.

Nevertheless, the growing interest in Europe in creating a more clear-cut role for the chair of the governing body has not yet led to any clear descriptions of the chairperson's role – apart from in a number of books and publications. We've seen references to the board chair here and there in various corporate governance codes but they don't contain very clear descriptions of the actual role to be fulfilled. Moreover, as far as I know, very little research has been done to date into how board chairs carry out their duties and how effectively they do so.

In the following sections, I'll describe, on the basis of my own experience, what a board chair should be able to do. Consequently, my description is based on the profile of a non-executive chair. In fact, the expression 'executive chairman' seems to me to be a contradiction in terms. I must also warn the reader that the job of the board chair as described here isn't necessarily valid for all companies. By this I don't mean to imply that the job is so company-specific that it differs from every company to every other company, but it is nevertheless the case that the role of chairperson simply cannot be identical at all companies. What I'm describing here are the generic elements of the job.

The role of the board of directors

The role of the board chair must inevitably be inferred from the core duties of the board of directors as a whole. In Chapter 1, I summarised these core duties in the form of a diamond. I indicated that these duties are four in number: setting the course which the organisation should follow; supervising/monitoring the management of the organisation; setting standards and promulgating corporate values; and taking responsibility/being accountable for what happens at the firm or organisation. I'm not going to discuss these core tasks here again, but I will draw out from them a number of subtasks that are of particular importance for the chairman or woman.

ENSURING THE RIGHT MANAGEMENT

A very important task – probably the most fundamental one – of a board of directors is to make sure that the executive management are doing their job well. Regrettably, I don't always see this task included in descriptions of what a board of directors and its chair do. This duty is of course dependent on the context in which the governing body operates, especially the shareholder structure. Where the company has a highly concentrated shareholder structure, the major shareholder will probably play a significant part in appointing the management, whereas at other firms it will be the board of directors that plays the central role in appraising current management and conducting a search for new management if that becomes necessary. It goes without saying that the board chair will play no small part in performing this first task.

ENSURING AN EFFECTIVE STRATEGY

A second task is to ensure that the company management is pursuing a strategy that's in line with the targets and objectives of the company and the shareholders and to monitor whether the strategy is being implemented in an efficient and effective manner. It's not the job of the board of directors to draw up the strategy – that's a job for management – but the board should nevertheless be called upon to green-light the strategy and the directors will subsequently have to judge whether the strategy is achieving the desired results. If this is not the case, then it will be up to the members of the board – and first and foremost the chair – to talk over the strategy again with the executive management. It's also part of the board's duty to hold a debate on the subject and, whenever necessary, to assess whether a different approach should be taken. I would underline once again that the chairperson and the other directors are not responsible for drawing up the strategy. They're not in a position to do so because they don't have the detailed knowledge that the management team has, but they must be able to judge whether the strategy is bringing about results within the agreed risk profile.

ENSURING THE AVAILABILITY AND PROPER USE OF RESOURCES

The board of directors must make efforts to ensure that the company has the resources to implement the agreed strategy. The board will therefore have to decide on such matters as a capital increase or reduction, taking out new loans and setting dividend policy. Obviously, the use made of these resources will have to be monitored and the board of directors will be accountable to the company's shareholders, bond-holders and banks that provided the resources. No particular task is assigned to the board chair in this field. In practice, it's the management's job to publish announcements of results and risks; the board's role is confined to supervising and monitoring the way this is carried out.

ASSUMING RESPONSIBILITY

Another important role for the board of directors is to assume responsibility for any contracts with or commitments to third parties into which the company enters. Ostensibly this is a rather administrative task but it's no less important for that reason. Managers delegated by the board to perform the necessary work will be able to take on a lot of the responsibility but they'll usually be expected to stay within specific guidelines pertaining to the delegated powers. The chair has no specific role here, although sometimes s/he will append his/her signature to the contract or commitment, thus confirming the board's official agreement vis-à-vis the third parties involved.

The role of the chair

Starting out from the role of the board of directors, we can now provide a more detailed description of the role of its chairman or woman. I set out below the tasks which – as a minimum – fall to the chairperson.

ENSURING THAT THE BOARD IS ABLE TO CARRY OUT ITS FUNCTIONS

The primary task of a board chair is to ensure that the board of directors actually performs its duties. I summarised above the four elements that make up the board's role. These are the starting point for the chair's job. S/he must ensure that meetings are held, supported by the relevant documents, to enable the directors to perform their duties. S/he must further ensure that proper deliberations take place at those meetings, during which all points of view are expressed and heard, that decisions are taken and that a report (the 'minutes') on the decision-making process is drawn up. Obviously, the chair doesn't have to do this all by him/herself but the company must provide him or her with the necessary resources and tools to carry out this basic task.

ENSURING THAT THE BOARD IS, AND REMAINS, ABLE TO MAKE DECISIONS

It's a very important part of the chair's job to ensure that the board actually reaches decisions. Proposals sent up to the board of directors by management must therefore be brought swiftly to a conclusion. This doesn't always have to be completed at a single meeting, but the governing body shouldn't hesitate endlessly over proposals tabled for decision. Of course, the directors don't necessarily have to approve each and every one of the proposals made by management.

If serious questions are voiced in the boardroom, the chair should make sure that management provides extra information or additional explanations.

In any case, indecision must be avoided. Sometimes indecision is simply the result of disagreement among the various board members. In such cases, the chair should try to find a compromise that's acceptable to a large majority of the directors and can also obtain the backing of the management. A particular problem can arise whenever the governing body rejects a management proposal. At such moments, the chairperson's wisdom will be put to the test: s/he will need to calm any tension that may arise between the directors on the one side and the executive management on the other. S/he may have to seek a compromise in order to repair any breakdown in trust that may appear. In an extreme case, it might be necessary to change the management team. These are all issues which, at the end of the day, it will be up to the chair to resolve.

> If the board is divided, it's up to the chair to try to find a compromise.

ORGANISING CORPORATE GOVERNANCE

Another important task for the chair is organising corporate governance at the company or organisation. I observe that some writers include this task among the CEO's responsibilities.[14] I'm always surprised when I see this. Corporate governance has a number of different aims, but the main goal is to ensure that the company is run in the interests of its shareholders and other stakeholders and that everyone's interests are fairly defended. You cannot leave this

---

14   In a number of publications discussing CEOs' performance, the pursuit of good corporate governance is explicitly mentioned as one of the CEO-appraisal criteria. However, there are good arguments for making this aspect part of the chair's responsibilities.

to the CEO; it's part of the responsibilities of the board of directors, which is formally accountable vis-à-vis third parties, and so it's clearly a matter for the chair.

CONTACT WITH SHAREHOLDERS

Day-to-day contact with shareholders, investors and analysts is handled by executive management, who have all the necessary information and knowledge of the business to enable them to answer any questions which people with a financial interest in the firm might ask. Nevertheless, it's quite useful for the chair to get in touch with the reference shareholder or major shareholders now and again to find out their strategic views with regard to the company. Do they intend to stay with the company? Do they want to go for an IPO on the stock market? What's their assessment of the company management and what has been their experience of contact with managers? These are all things which the chair ought to be aware of if s/he doesn't want to have any nasty surprises. S/he should also be in a position to anticipate possible tension between, or conflicts of interest among, shareholders. The chair should preferably, as far as possible, work with the management on these issues but should also be in a position to take on the role of trusted confidant should any problems arise.

CONTACT WITH DIRECTORS

A board chair must know the minds of the other board members. S/he must know or be able to sense what they think and what they want. If one of the directors makes a remark or asks a question at a board meeting which comes as a surprise to the chairman or woman, this means that s/he has probably failed somewhere. Regular contact outside the boardroom between chair and individual directors can serve as a useful source of information – not least regarding what directors think of the management. Do board members have full confidence in the management or do they have doubts? These are important questions to which the chair must know the answers if s/he wants to avoid problems in the boardroom. S/he also needs to know whether the directors are united behind the strategic direction and decisions which the company will need to take. If this isn't the case, then s/he will have to look for compromises, either working together with the CEO or, if necessary, alone.

APPRAISAL OF DIRECTORS

The chair must take the leading role in assessing the performance of the board and the individual directors – which of course includes his or her own performance. In order to conduct an appraisal of his/her own work, s/he may have to call in external experts but should give a central role in this process to fellow directors.

GRASP OF COMPANY STRATEGY AND STRATEGIC CHALLENGES

The chair needs to be the best informed of all board members as regards the company strategy and the strategic challenges it faces. S/he must also be able to make a credible independent assessment of what the company needs to do in order to develop the business and keep growing. S/he will not announce this assessment to the outside world as if s/he were the CEO, but will nonetheless have his/her own judgement as to whether the enterprise is heading in the right direction and taking the right steps to cope with a changing economic situation. This approach will enable the chairperson to act as a coach to the chief executive.

KNOWING THE COMPANY'S KEY STAFF

More than any of the other directors, the board chair must get to know all important employees at the company, be aware of how well they work together and be able to judge the contribution they're making towards achieving the company's objectives and targets. S/he must have a feel for their ambitions and should try to form an independent opinion about their career opportunities. S/he won't of course be able to do so without discussing such matters with the CEO and certainly shouldn't go around spying on the organisation. Nevertheless, there are a lot of informal, yet fully transparent, ways of getting to know people. If there's good cooperation between chair and CEO, they'll be able to help and support each other in the vital process of identifying talent.

Another reason for keeping in touch with key staff and other employees at the company is that this is a good way for the board chair to keep up with what's happening inside the firm. Such valuable insights may help to prevent friction arising in the organisation but this process must not be allowed to turn into a sort of gossip factory. Job appointments are primarily a matter for the management – unless we're talking about the post of CEO or other top executive positions. However, when the chair knows the key people quite well, this can prove extremely useful if one day the company is facing management succession problems. It's always a good idea for the company directors, especially the chair, to know the people who might well be running the business in the future.

ACTING AS 'LAST RESORT' FOR WHISTLEBLOWERS

Who can whistleblowers turn to? Any modern organisation has procedures and people in place for this purpose. But what happens if it all goes awry and the people concerned don't know where to turn? In such exceptional cases, the board chair can sometimes play a useful role. However, it is advisable that, once a complaint or expression of dissatisfaction has come to the ears of the chairman or woman, s/he should channel the matter through an objective procedure as quickly as possible in order to avoid becoming involved as a concerned party in the dispute.

PROMOTING IN-DEPTH DELIBERATIONS

A very important substantive task for any chairman or woman is to ensure that all proposals for decision receive in-depth consideration. S/he must have sufficient knowledge of the issues to be able to follow the points being discussed at board meetings. I don't mean that s/he should constantly thrust his/her own opinions into the debate but s/he must be able to judge whether any given remark is serious and well-founded, and whether any proposals or solutions put forward by a director are based on expert knowledge. S/he should moreover bring as many board members as possible into the discussion, broadening and deepening the deliberations so that all points of view and all pros and cons are heard, prior to making a decision.

TAKING THE INITIATIVE IF THINGS GO WRONG

Sometimes the unexpected may happen and things may go wrong with the company strategy or the management. At such moments, the board chair must be able to take the initiative. If I appear to be stating the obvious, it's worth pointing out that s/he will only be able to do so if she can correctly assess the seriousness of the situation and quickly set out the various options for the board to consider. The situation may indeed take a very serious turn if the company is faced with rapidly deteriorating financial circumstances or even a takeover bid. At that moment, the chair must, as it were, play the fireman.

If things go wrong, the chair needs to act like a fireman, making the right decisions under time pressure.

When the flames are getting hot, you often need to make a choice between a short-term and a longer-term solution. That kind of decision is not always easy to make under extreme time pressure.

HAVING A FEEL FOR TIMING

It's generally accepted that the chair will have a big hand in drawing up the agenda for meetings of the board of directors. This isn't just a simple matter of listing all the points that might appear on the next agenda. It's much more important that s/he should have a good feel for the timing. When is the right moment to discuss a given issue such as appointing new directors or planning management team succession? When should the company strategy be looked at again? When is it appropriate to address the question of a capital increase or talk again about possible mergers and acquisitions? To deal with these questions, the board chair needs to know what the most important shareholders think about those issues.

To sum up

A good, balanced division of responsibilities between chair and CEO is crucial for the efficient operation of the company and for good corporate governance. Even today, still very little is known about what exactly the role of the board chair should be and how s/he should perform his/her duties. This is certainly a subject that ought to receive greater attention in the future. In this chapter I've attempted to set out a number of elements – based on my own personal experiences and observations – that will perhaps be useful in helping the chair of a governing body to fulfil his or her duties. I hope at least that the considerations I've put forward will encourage board chairs and chief executives to start talking about how those working in these two posts could cooperate more effectively.

CHAPTER 7

Tension at the top

Why each director should concentrate on his/her allotted task

At the top of any company or organisation, you'll find a group of people with their own interests, ambitions and ideas who have come together to achieve a certain aim. This combination often leads to disunity. So, from time to time tension will arise – between chair and CEO, between the CEO and the management, and among individual managers or directors. What can cause such tension and how can it be avoided?

IT'S NOT UNUSUAL TO FIND STRESSES AND STRAINS AT THE TOP OF AN organisation. Talented and ambitious people who are called upon to work in one or more teams all have their own ideas about what the common vision should be. However, they have the task, either as individuals or jointly as a team, of achieving part of that vision. To turn a vision into reality, you need to work out a strategy and there may be a lack of unity on this as well. The greatest source of disunity is however the allocation of resources: who receives how much?

Any person working in the top echelons of a company will usually be happy to take on his/her allotted task and also, if at all possible, expand it. In any case, those individuals will fight tooth and nail to hang on to the responsibilities assigned to them and they'll regard the compensation they receive for taking on those responsibilities as either insufficient or fairly good, but very rarely too high! They'll also of course have their own ambitions as to what they want to achieve at the company or in their private lives. Some managers may have their minds set on becoming head of the entire organisation.

In a nutshell, there's a lot of potential for conflict at the top of an organisation. The governing body needs to be aware of this and also to realise not only that tension is nothing abnormal but that it may even be productive for the organisation, because tension at the top can provide the impetus required to perform well.

Tension between chair and chief executive

In principle, there shouldn't be any tension between the board chair and the CEO. Nevertheless, friction can arise, and does so perhaps more often than the outside world might imagine because it's usually kept well hidden. In the following sections, I will outline four possible causes: personalities that don't work well together, don't recognise each other's individual roles or are unwilling to work according to those roles; differences of opinion on strategy, results, management, employees or investments; reluctance to see the other person enjoying more of the limelight; and dissatisfaction with remuneration.

PERSONALITIES THAT FIND IT HARD TO WORK WELL TOGETHER

One obvious explanation for friction arising between the board chair and the chief executive is that their personalities aren't really compatible. A hands-on chairman or woman will often come into conflict with a CEO who can't easily tolerate the chair involving him/herself in operational matters. This is why I would argue that a former CEO will not always be the right person to chair a board, and certainly not if the person who's about to take over the chair is the predecessor of the current CEO. In such cases, s/he'll need to accept the change of role. Meanwhile the new CEO will always feel that the chair thinks s/he knows better because of his/her experience and operational know-how.

I therefore feel it's better if the chair and the CEO are people with different characters. I accept that this is a rather theoretical view and that a lot of counter-arguments might be brought against it but I genuinely think I'm right about this. At the risk of making the personality differences too much of a caricature, I think it's better that the chair should have no inclination for operational matters, or at least not be someone who gets a kick out of solving operational problems or directly managing staff. The chair must first and foremost be interested in conceptualising problems, assessing people and motivating managers. The CEO should also score well on the last two points, of course, but should normally have a greater inclination towards finding practical solutions to problems rather than conceptualising them.

Some experiments have actually been conducted, whereby specific tasks were formally allocated to the CEO on the one hand and the board chair on the other. I've had the opportunity to observe at close quarters how a number of these agreements worked out in practice and I'm not convinced that they can work. I think the best thing is for the chairperson to stick to what I've described in Chapter 6 and let the CEO get on with his/her job. However, friction between the two officers can only really be prevented if each recognises that s/he has a distinct role to play in the company or organisation, so that the chair will help the CEO to do his/her executive job properly and the CEO will support the chair as s/he endeavours to fulfil his/her duties. This will require, among other things, open, transparent communication and mutual respect between the two.

DIFFERENCES OF OPINION ON STRATEGY, RESULTS, MANAGEMENT, EMPLOYEES, OR INVESTMENTS

Too similar personalities can lead to tension, but there are other factors that may disturb relations at the top of the organisation, the most obvious

When differences of opinion drag on, this is often a symptom of a deeper-lying conflict.

being substantive differences of opinion. Different individuals will often have different views about other people or on what they think ought to be done in a given situation. However, such differences need not lead to long, drawn-out conflicts – or at least not if the CEO, the chair and the other board members behave properly towards each other. If such conflicts do drag on for a long time, it's more often a sign of deeper-lying conflicts that have to do with personalities and roles in the organisation – i.e. it's basically all about whether the CEO and the chair recognise and respect each other's roles.

THE LIMELIGHT

Sometimes the board chairman or woman will receive more attention in the press than the chief executive. This might simply be because s/he's more of a public figure whom journalists find it easier to call on the phone. It's actually better if the chair doesn't make any comment in such situations, except in a crisis or when it's really necessary to do so. On the other hand, it can also happen that the chairperson isn't happy to see the company CEO receiving constant attention in the news media or social media. A chairman or woman who has had a long public career may need to practice a little modesty here. S/he may perhaps be able to play an advisory role vis-à-vis the chief executive, provided that the CEO thinks this is useful and doesn't find it patronising. I think the most sensible thing would be for the two officers to talk openly about it and, whenever useful, agree on a division of responsibilities for specific events such as annual meetings, works parties or major interviews.

DISSATISFACTION WITH REMUNERATION OR BONUSES

The board chair is often the main point of contact for the CEO when it comes to compensation and bonuses. Even at companies with a formal remuneration committee, the chair will sometimes quickly be drawn into the discussions. This is never an easy exercise. The CEO may clearly express his/her expectations as regards fixed salary and bonus or may be less outspoken about it. The silent scenario is of course the most difficult, because then figuring out what the

CEO actually wants for him/herself and the company workforce is largely a matter of guesswork. If the chairperson hesitates, the CEO is likely to accuse him/her and the other board members of not showing sufficient respect for the work that has been performed. This isn't very good for collaboration at the company. On the other hand, a too-generous attitude on the part of the chair is not so good either because it's bad for cost management and may draw criticism from the shareholders or the general public. It's easy to state that the company needs to seek a balanced solution but what exactly does this balanced solution consist of? Catchphrases such as "management compensation must be in line with the market" have some use as general principles, but the actual situation is different for every CEO and every management team. The best way to avoid tension around remuneration is to hold a clear, open discussion about the CEO's expectations and make it clear what can reasonably be done and what is defensible vis-à-vis shareholders or public opinion. This whole subject can nevertheless be a source of concealed tension, especially if the management team have the feeling that not everyone is being treated in the same way.

Those are four factors that may give rise to friction between chair and CEO. If the friction does not abate, then it's clear that either the chief executive or the chairperson will have to leave. At listed companies, this kind of problem can lead to long, drawn-out conflict. At companies with a highly concentrated shareholder structure, the choice between CEO and chairperson will be made quite quickly. In this type of conflict, it's not easy to predict who will emerge the winner, or who will survive. I've seen quite a few examples of where the chairperson remained in post but I've also seen the reverse happen. There are too many one-off factors at play here to allow us to arrive at a general theory as to who will win a battle between chair and CEO.

Tension between CEO and management or among managers

Tensions in the management committee or executive committee are often well concealed and hardly perceptible to the governing body. To my eternal shame, I myself was once involved in a situation that perfectly illustrates this. Years ago, I received a phone call on a Wednesday evening from the chairman of the governing body to request my attendance at an emergency meeting that very evening. The company's entire management team had resigned, leaving the CEO no choice but to resign himself. This was a painful situation for all concerned, but very much so for the governing body and the chairman since none of the directors had any idea that a high degree of friction had arisen between the chief executive and the rest of the management, and neither the CEO himself or any of the managers had told us anything about it. So the governing body found itself without any executive management in place. That was a highly unusual situation and I've only been involved in such circumstances once in my career, but the example shows how a conflict among company management can smoulder on unresolved for months until it suddenly bursts into flames. Eventually, we found a solution by hiring a new CEO but it was still a particularly difficult and painful period for the governing body.

I can point to five factors which can cause conflict to arise in a management team: doubts about the CEO's leadership capacity; differences of opinion on strategy; dissatisfaction with remuneration; ambitions to succeed the current CEO; and personality conflicts.

DOUBTS ABOUT THE CEO'S LEADERSHIP

This is probably the most frequent reason for conflicts among company management. Managers begin to doubt the CEO's leadership if they observe that s/he hesitates to step in and take action when results are on the slide or tolerates poor performance by a fellow manager. Likewise, if the CEO is unwilling to engage in sufficient consultation with managers on the policies to be followed or gives different messages to different members of the executive board so that managers have the impression that they're being set up in opposition to each other, this can lead to large-scale resistance.

DIFFERENCES OF OPINION ON STRATEGY

There will always be discussions about the strategy the company ought to be following, the vision to be attained and on the question of who obtains what level of resources in order to bring the strategy to fruition. This doesn't have to create major friction. The discussions in the management board will usually be tough but open and frank. Hidden tension arises if managers get the feeling that the CEO is no longer capable of keeping the debate on track and resolving the thorny points. Managers are usually prepared to give way in a strategy discussion if the CEO shows leadership and points the way forward. If s/he doesn't show such leadership, hidden tensions begin to brew, which will cause problems at some point in time.

DISSATISFACTION WITH REMUNERATION

Managers expect to receive a variable compensation package in line with the results achieved and the efforts they've made to meet the targets set. The remuneration committee does of course play a role here but it's the CEO who will draw up proposals for managers' variable compensation and the committee will usually follow those proposals. Not following the CEO's proposals can come across as a sign of lack of trust, although at many companies it's actually up to the remuneration committee to fix the principles for determining variable compensation. If one or more managers don't agree with their appraisals and the variable compensation they've received from the CEO, this can be the start of rising tensions among the management. Some CEOs try to resolve this problem by allocating exactly the same variable compensation to all the management but this approach might, once again, be regarded as unfair as it doesn't properly reward the best-performing managers.

AMBITIONS TO SUCCEED THE CURRENT CEO

Whenever the end of a CEO's mandate approaches or if it becomes clear to a number of managers that s/he isn't working in optimal fashion or no longer enjoys the full confidence of the governing body or the shareholders, competition will arise between those managers who think they're in the running to take over the CEO role. The existence of a succession plan doesn't usually suppress the competition because those plans rarely end up being implemented as originally drawn up. Board members should take care not to be used as tools in this contest for the CEO job. It's advisable for the board to act swiftly and in a resolute manner to decide the succession question.

PERSONALITY CONFLICTS

Just as conflicts of personality can arise between the chair and the chief executive, such conflicts may also arise between the CEO and the management. However, I think this is less of a problem among the management because if the CEO is a good leader, s/he will select managers with whom s/he will be able to work well. If things don't work out, it's much easier for the chief executive to do something about the conflict: s/he can switch the manager in question over to another task or ask him/her to 'seek other opportunities' elsewhere.

Tension in the governing body

Tensions can also of course arise between board members. Directors are first and foremost responsible for promoting the interests of the company or organisation. However, they may also be representing the interests of particular shareholders or a reference shareholder. Friction may arise because various decisions may change the position of those shareholders. For instance, a capital increase to which not all shareholders are able to subscribe will seriously alter the balance of power and influence at the company. Even the valuation of a company ahead of a capital increase can have a serious impact. Differences of opinion may also arise over dividend policy, especially at family businesses, where the various branches of the family may have differing views about dividend distribution. Some will prefer to retain funds within the company while others will want to pocket a dividend so as to be able to invest the money elsewhere or spend it.

There are thus many kinds of decisions that may bring the differing interests of various different shareholders into sharp focus and so will not fail to have an impact on the discussions in the governing body. These will not usually provoke long-lasting conflicts, because solutions will have to be found. Nevertheless, at a family-owned company, you need to take care that any intra-family differences of opinion don't spill over into the boardroom. A lot of family-owned firms

> At a family company you need to prevent family rows spilling over into the boardroom.

have set up structures to ensure that family disputes don't hamper the functioning of the board. Creating a family council can provide a vehicle for talking through and clearing up any problems. In any case, even if a family dispute arises, the board chair must endeavour to ensure that the governing body can go on working and that its meetings don't become a pure formality where the directors are no longer able to fulfil their course-setting and supervisory duties properly.

To sum up

Directors must always be aware that there is a chance of conflict arising at the top of a company or organisation at any time. It's vital to be able to spot conflicts in good time or, even better, anticipate them. Both the board chair and the CEO have an essential role to play in finding a solution. It's very important to analyse the conflict thoroughly, based on good information and careful consideration, but it's equally important to be able to find a powerful solution that can be rapidly applied. Allowing a problem to run on without any solution or with a half-solution is of no benefit whatsoever to a company or organisation.

CHAPTER 8

Managing your ignorance

How directors can find out what they need to know

A governing body is supposed to do everything necessary to achieve the purpose and targets of the company or organisation. However, a board of directors that meets only a few times a year certainly cannot know about everything that's been happening inside the organisation. So how can the directors cope with their ignorance and manage to fulfil their duties?

I REMEMBER A CONVERSATION I HAD WITH A PERSON ALONGSIDE whom I'd been sitting on the board of directors at a company for a long time and who one day had been asked by his fellow directors to replace the existing chief executive. After a few weeks in the job, he said: "I've been sitting on the board of directors of this company for years but now that I've become the CEO, it's just as if I'd walked into a different company. Everything's different from what I'd thought." I assume that there's some degree of exaggeration in this declaration. But still... the view you have of a company or organisation does of course depend on where you're standing. Members of the governing body will have a different angle of view than the management, and the workforce on the shop floor will have a different picture again. It's interesting that the picture varies according to your level in the organisation, and the board of directors should take this into account when they're making decisions. However, the most important thing for the directors is to be able to obtain the information and insights they need to carry out their course-setting and supervision duties properly. There are various different channels they can use.

CEO and management: the first point of contact

The directors should in the first instance be informed by the CEO about all the ins and outs of the company or organisation and about the issues which the organisation is having to deal with at all levels. If it's about a technical aspect that is nonetheless highly relevant for the board of directors, such as cybersecurity, the CEO will quite easily be able to have the information forwarded by the manager responsible for that subject. Board members of course remain free to approach any member of the management with their questions, but it's discourteous not to let the CEO know about this and directors should in fact inform the board chair whenever they get in touch with managers. The CEO and the chairperson both have a right to know whom directors are contacting, so that they can help to channel things in the right way – not so as to manage the content of the information collection efforts but to ensure that, apart from fulfilling their duty to provide information, the managers are left to get on with their jobs. This is also the reason why direct contact between directors and management outside meetings of the governing body should remain the exception, be conducted through the normal channels, and certainly avoid undermining the authority of the chief executive.

The precept that board members should 'hold back' a little vis-à-vis the company management is of course no longer applicable if it should become clear that there's a serious management problem at the company. In that case, however, the directors should act in a coordinated way, ideally under the leadership of the chair. The board of directors is supposed to be a collective body so it makes no sense for every director to take his/her own separate initiatives to obtain information about the state of affairs at the company.

The information which the governing body expects, under normal circumstances, to receive from the CEO and the management team relates to the company's commercial and financial results, any changes in the market, cost evolution, the firm's competitive position, compliance with legal and regulatory requirements, actual and planned investment, and any problems which the company is facing now, or may face in the future. The relevant figures will normally be provided smoothly and flawlessly. Should that not be the case, there's probably something seriously wrong.

Communication about problems with which the company is struggling can often be rather more awkward. The CEO and the management team certainly don't enjoy having to admit that problems have arisen. Of course, the governing body doesn't necessarily have to be informed about every little problem; only those issues that fall within the remit of the board of directors should be passed up to the directors for discussion. Failure to hit the financial targets, a financial problem that has arisen because a major customer is unable to pay its debts to the company, snags with product development, headwinds in some market segments, a major lawsuit brought against the company, the resignation or dismissal of a senior manager – these are all examples of subjects on which the board must be kept up to date. This isn't an exhaustive list. If there's a high degree of trust between the governing body and the CEO, this type of problem will automatically be relayed to the directors. However, if a climate of suspicion prevails, such matters may be hushed up or not reported in good time.

Another problem that can take time to filter through to the directors is the existence of quarrels or serious tension in the executive board or management team. Fortunately, this sort of thing doesn't happen very often, but when it does happen the consequences are usually very serious. Interpersonal friction is not something that gets reported very easily – and when it does come out it's usually too late to do anything about it. If the CEO is the only member of the executive with a seat on the governing body, it's hard for the other directors to find out that things are not going smoothly in the management team, especially as executives tend not to air their grievances openly. Below I offer some tips on how to detect and deal with this kind of problem.

> **When problems within the executive management land on the boardroom table, it's usually too late.**

Committees can serve as antennae

Committees reporting to the board of directors can serve as antennae, picking up on things that are going on in the organisation. Only directors officially have seats on the various committees, but other members of the organisation also sometimes take part in their meetings, so the committees tend to collect more information – and faster – than the full board is able to do. This can give the directors a better view of how the company is performing and the risks it's running.

The audit committee has the opportunity to obtain more information about the company from the internal auditors. This information can be very broad in nature, enabling the directors to see for instance how well the IT department is performing or examine company procurement policy. This kind of data doesn't however reveal the more strategic issues or raise questions about the corporate culture. Moreover, the information collected and reported to the audit committee is usually retrospective, showing what has happened rather than providing clues as to what is expected to happen going forward.

The audit and risk committee meetings are attended by specialist advisors such as external auditors and legal experts. The external auditors have a specific task: to ensure that the accounts provide a true and fair view of the current state and performance of the company. Consequently, the external auditors are essentially expected to give their stamp of approval to the figures which the board members will be using in order to make an assessment of the company or organisation. However, they may also indicate points which the board might find useful to discuss with management, such as asset valuations and provisions for future liabilities. This makes it harder for anyone to 'doctor' the figures in order to present a more favourable picture. The company legal officer is also there to provide the directors with insights into potential legal risks which the company or organisation might face, and how serious those risks are.

Not all companies have an internal auditor and an in-house lawyer. Fortunately, those that don't are usually smaller firms. In any case, directors at smaller enterprises have a better view of what's happening and the shareholders are generally more closely involved with the business.

Benchmarking

Another way to obtain a picture of what's happening at the company is to compare the key figures with those of one of your competitors or a similar kind of business. This process is quite similar to what doctors do when they carry out a patient diagnosis. They'll measure blood pressure and take a blood sample for analysis. They then compare these various key indicators with those of a normal healthy person. A doctor who detects any discrepancies will then take a further look to find out what exactly is wrong with the patient.

You can do something similar with a company. Once the directors have compared the company's key figures with those of other firms – a process known as benchmarking – they'll be in a position to ask questions about whether something is going wrong. Suppose that revenues are growing more slowly than those of the competitors or that inventory turnover is too low or revenue per employee is down. The question is then why this is the case. An efficient CEO and management team will already have carried out this analysis themselves and should be able to answer these questions quite easily. If they can't, that speaks volumes about the efficiency of the management team. This example is intended to show how directors can get to know a lot about the company or organisation without going around interfering directly in its day-to-day workings.

The chairperson's involvement

All the instruments to help obtain a clearer insight into the operations of the company that I've discussed so far are firmly based on quantitative information. So how can the board of directors obtain insights into the corporate culture, management-workforce relations, company dynamics, management conduct, and strategic challenges? These are all unquestionably important elements that will have an impact on the company's current and future results.

I've already discussed the role of the board chair in a previous chapter, but I'd just like to add a few remarks on the subject here. A chairperson doesn't – except under very rare circumstances – need to play an executive role at the company, but s/he must be closely involved. By this, I mean that s/he must have a feel for how the company is doing, what the strategic challenges and opportunities are, how the managers are performing, which of them are top performers and which of them are finding it harder to fulfil their tasks, and consequently who might potentially be in line for promotion. Without wishing to be a busybody, the chairman or woman must ensure that adequate informal contacts take place within the organisation. This is the only way s/he'll be able to form an opinion about the corporate culture – relations between the various managers, for instance. And she'll only be able to absorb this kind of 'soft' information if s/he avoids coming across as a martinet or inspector. As I stressed earlier, the chairperson must try not to be seen as a spy sent by the board. I would suggest that any chairperson needs two basic skills: knowing how to ask the right questions and being a good listener.

Works visits

I think it's very important to go and visit a division or department of the company or organisation now and again. This kind of visit provides you with a direct impression of how things are really going.

As a director, you can learn a lot from this, provided the management haven't 'staged' your visit too tightly. I think that this kind of visit is particularly useful if you have the opportunity to find out about a new development, a new service, or an activity that has been reorganised. This will give you a better insight into things than just reading the board meeting documents. Another benefit of a works visit is that it shows employees that the directors and the management take real interest in what they're doing.

Listening to customers and third parties

Last but not least, board members can obtain useful information by listening attentively to what company employees, customers and suppliers have to say about their experiences with the firm. You can do so at any chance meeting that occurs. I don't mean that the board chair ought to be planning formal meetings with employees, customers and suppliers – which might well lead to confusion over the respective roles of the chair and CEO. During such chance or casual encounters, it's very important to listen very carefully because the comments people make are not always entirely disinterested and may contain as much noise as information. However, sometimes very useful things emerge from remarks made on such occasions.

Perhaps an example will help to clarify what I mean. Some time ago, I was sitting talking with a customer of a company where I served as a member of the board. The customer was complaining that a particular service was no longer available. Luckily enough, I happened to know that this service was in fact still available but not in all locations. It wasn't my job to explain this to the customer – although I might well choose to do so out of simple courtesy – this ought to be the responsibility of the sales department. Anyway, this provided me with an opportunity to talk to the CEO about how customers receive such information and whether the firm's sales communication was efficient enough. It's more useful when company directors ask general questions about how things work than when they try to solve specific shortcomings.

To sum up

Board members are supposed to set the course for the organisation and provide supervision, but they tend to have too little information. In this chapter, I've indicated some of the various ways in which directors can obtain the information they need in order to carry out their duties. This kind of information will not be detailed or exhaustive, but if the board is doing its job properly, it will meet the directors' needs adequately.

CHAPTER 9

How to become, and remain, a good director

Many feel the call...

"How can I become a company director?" This is a question I've heard dozens of times. Most of the time, I'm at a loss for an answer because there are so many factors that determine whether a person will be appointed a member of a board or governing body. However, it's much easier to describe accurately what it takes to become a good director.

How does someone become a director? And how does it come about that some directors have seats on several governing bodies, while other people find it hard to obtain even a single mandate or fail to obtain any board appointment at all? I cannot give precise answers to these questions, as there are a lot of factors that play a part in the appointment of a director.

How do you become a director?

One important aspect is that board appointments are subject to seasonal factors. That may sound strange, but it's true. Directors are elected at the annual general meeting (AGM) of shareholders, which takes place only once a year, usually in spring, so consequently most directorial appointments are made during that period. There are exceptions to this general rule. Board members can also be elected at an extraordinary general meeting (EGM) but this is certainly not common practice.

> It may sound strange, but appointments to a board of directors are seasonal.

There are basically three possible reasons why a vacancy arises on a governing body. The first is when a director's mandate comes to an end. Either the director in question doesn't want to have his/her mandate extended, or is unable to accept a renewal because s/he has reached the statutory limit for renewal, or there isn't a consensus at the top of the organisation to extend the mandate. A second scenario is that a director steps down before the expiry of the mandate, for personal reasons, because s/he wants to go and do something else or a serious conflict of interest with his/her other activities has arisen. Thirdly, a vacancy may arise because the board of directors decides that representation on the governing body needs to be broadened. There may be various reasons for this decision: they want to bring in new expertise; an important new shareholder has come on board; or, as part of a takeover deal, an agreement was reached that the newly-acquired company will have representation on the board of the acquirer.

Directors can also be dismissed instantly following a vote at the AGM but this hardly ever happens because it's very difficult to make one individual accountable for poor governance. However, there are individual errors of behaviour, such as misuse of company funds, or making unfair use of privileged information for personal gain – known as 'insider trading' – for which a director can be blamed.

These examples show that board members aren't just continuously appointed and that in a significant number of cases directors are representing certain shareholder interests. In listed companies with a fragmented shareholder structure, shareholders have a lesser influence on directorial appointments. At non-listed companies with a limited number of shareholders, it's quite obvious that the shareholders will have a large say in the appointment and re-appointment of board members. Anyone who wishes to become a director will therefore have to take account of the seasonal effect and the influence of particular shareholders.

In order to find a director to fill a vacant seat on the governing body, the board can call upon one of the specialist search consultancies. This mainly happens if a company wants to bring in a foreign director or perhaps to approach a candidate without letting him or her know immediately from which firm the enquiry is coming. This gives both parties the chance to think about the proposal without commitment and enables the company to compare several candidates. However, quite a lot of board seats are filled without the aid of a professional search advisor. The informal network of directors and shareholders still plays a part in such processes, though some people deplore this approach. Personally, I think that a good method of recruiting a suitable board member is a combination of professional search and good networking. The reasons are obvious. Directors don't owe their seats on the board exclusively to their specialist knowledge; they need to be able to work together and, above all, be available whenever the company is in difficulty. It does actually happen that when a company is heading for a crisis, directors who aren't closely involved will disengage and make their apologies when a meeting is called, or else show up with their lawyers. This is perhaps a clever approach when it comes to shielding yourself from liability but it doesn't really help the company to move forward.

> You can recruit good directors by combining networking with professional research.

Proposals have been made to the effect that board members should only be appointed after they've passed an examination or obtained certification. This may perhaps be useful for corporations in some complex fields, such as banking or nuclear energy, but to make this a general requirement seems to me to be going too far. Proponents of this idea place emphasis on individual specialist knowledge required by board members, whereas to my mind they're paying far too little attention to the fact that a governing body needs to be able to function as a collective.

Candidates for a board seat also need to ask themselves whether they really want to become a director. 'Wannabe'-directors often think that they will have a more meaningful role at a company or non-profit organisation as a member of the governing body than as a manager. Usually, that's not true. Directors get to analyse, assess, advise and – in conjunction with their board colleagues – take decisions but, all in all, the job is fairly remote from the practical running of the organisation. As a director, you don't have your hands on the steering wheel. Not all board candidates realise this and they then sometimes end up disappointed about 'how little' they're able to achieve sitting on the governing body. Anyone who likes hands-on activity and wants to have the steering wheel in their hands shouldn't be trying to obtain a board seat but should preferably go looking for an executive job. It's a bit like the difference between a member of parliament and a government minister. Lots of politicians get more satisfaction out of working as a minister or local mayor than occupying a seat in parliament.

Leading specialists in a particular professional field often end up very disillusioned with the work of a governing body. Their special expertise is of course not required at every meeting and if, as a director, you don't have sufficient general understanding and experience to be able to talk about the other matters on the agenda, things can very quickly start to go wrong. In short, anyone who wants to be a member of a governing body must be able to work well together with others in a group, will have to be capable of standing back from the day-to-day management of the enterprise and will need to have broad general knowledge or experience.

How can you become a good director?

How can a director perform his/her duties well? Over the years, I've had the opportunity to observe a large number of directors and to try to work out how a director can have the greatest impact on the company or organisation.

As a starting point, it's important to differentiate between the interests that the director is – so to speak – defending and the overall interests of the company or non-profit organisation itself. As we saw in an earlier chapter, directors are often nominated by a group of shareholders, especially at an unlisted company. So board members may get the idea that they're there first and foremost to defend the interests of those shareholders. This attitude is perfectly understandable, but wrong.

The first duty of a director is to strive to achieve the purpose which the company or organisation has set itself. This is of course no simple task. On the one hand you've been appointed on the recommendation of

A director of a state-run company who thinks s/he represents a political party is taking the wrong view.

a group of shareholders, on the other hand you're (jointly) responsible for the enterprise as a whole, and as a director you'll have to find a balance between the two considerations. In previous chapters I've repeatedly emphasised that the governing body has collective rather than individual responsibility. Every director needs to be aware of this. The issue of what is in the company's interest versus the shareholders' plans may sometimes be felt keenly in state-run companies, where directors often wrongly imagine that they represent a political party on the board. They may think this, but from a legal viewpoint they're wholly mistaken: as soon as they accept a seat on the governing body, they're required by law to put the interests of the company first.

It's important that directors come to meetings well prepared. It's reasonable to expect that they've read the relevant documents thoroughly. A governing body cannot hold a meaningful discussion if the directors haven't studied the papers provided. This is why many regulators and oversight bodies in the financial world urge directors to take sufficient time during their mandate to read through heavy complex meeting documents thoroughly.

Unfortunately some directors only read their files for the first time when they arrive at the meeting.

Unfortunately, it happens quite often that directors only open their envelope of documents at the meeting itself – a clear sign that they haven't done their preparation. This isn't very encouraging for the managers who have put the documents together, and it doesn't make for a fruitful discussion. Moreover, electronic documents make it easier for directors to hide the fact that they haven't read the documents, although nowadays there are technical mechanisms for tracing whether or not a document has actually been consulted.

Directors must try to understand the real issues the company is facing. In their previous careers, they will perhaps have developed a certain way of thinking and will apply this approach to every problem or challenge. They need to realise that issues always differ from what was expected and that creative analysis can work wonders.

Directors are supposed to ask questions. We've already looked at the different approaches taken by the 'talkers' on the governing body on the one hand and the 'quieter ones' on the other. In every case, a director is expected to give his/her opinion in a decisive, but friendly, manner. Managers and colleagues are quick to spot when a person continually 'beats about the bush' and fails to come to the point. Directors who take an active part in the discussion – and this should apply to all of them – should not go into too much detail. That's always best left to the CEO and the management, who will have a better grasp of the background and be able to make better judgements when it comes to the details. Moreover, directors should not try to compete with managers as regards their respective capabilities. Former managers who obtain a board seat, even at a different company, should not seek to trump current managers with arguments such as: "I always did it such and such a way..." That kind of discussion inevitably leads to friction and solves very little. Directors should not aim to be 'back-seat drivers' in the management sphere.

Directors must also not forget that they're expected to maintain secrecy. A director must not repeat outside a governing body meeting whatever is said or decided there. Nor should s/he let anything slip to particular shareholders. Especially at companies where public authorities are the reference shareholder, mistakes are sometimes made when it comes to confidentiality. However, information leaks from the board of directors are the exception rather than the rule. It's therefore all the more regrettable when it does happen because it calls into question the credibility of all the board members.

Good directors make a difference

In my view there are four things that directors can do in order to make a significant impact on the way a company or organisation works and performs: cut through the traditional way of thinking about problems; formulate comments and ask questions that no-one has dared to ask up to that point in time; help to ensure more objective decision-making; and bring in know-how from other companies and markets.

CUTTING THROUGH TRADITIONAL WAYS OF THINKING

Companies and organisations become accustomed to addressing problems and challenges in the same way every time. There's often a lot to be said in favour of this approach. Everyone knows what has to be done and so the risks are lower. However, it's sometimes useful to deviate from the traditional way of doing things in order to contemplate something completely different. Let's take for example declining or stagnating book sales. How has this come about: a cyclical decline in the market, changes in people's reading behaviour? Or is it because of the advent of digital books? The traditional reaction from publishers would be: let's start by doing some promotion. Giving discounts on books. If you buy two books, you get a third free. These typical reactions are virtually hard-wired into the organisation: when sales fall, of course you have to step up your sales activities!

Directors can play a role in helping management to mull over what's really happening. Is it just a cyclical decline or is there something more serious going on? In this example, the answer is obvious. But I've learned that it's not all that easy to reach a consensus on what the real causes are and on the appropriate response. My example from the publishing sector is purely an illustration; you'll find similar problems at every company.

You will not however promote innovative thinking by constantly referring to what happens at similar companies or talking about "what we always used to do". Directors who always give the impression that things were better elsewhere or in the old days tend to lose credibility very quickly in the eyes of management. The task of the directors is not to import solutions from elsewhere; instead, they should strive to think creatively together about what the best approach might be for the firm on whose board they're currently sitting. Creative thinking about the specific problems the company is facing is vital not only for the company but also for any director's credibility.

FORMULATING BOLD REMARKS OR QUESTIONS

A second way in which directors can help a company or organisation to function more effectively and achieve more is by formulating bold remarks or questions. Many directors are rather conservative and will only ask questions that have known answers; they don't wish to be outliers in the governing body's discussion. Mostly they're afraid that their question will appear foolish. However, I've discovered that a director who dares to ask a pertinent question usually pinpoints the real issue. A governing body that is called upon to decide on the introduction of a risky product will usually be told that all the necessary research has been done and that all risks are known and calculated. Nevertheless, now and again there'll be a director who asks a really searching question, wanting to know what'll happen if the ECB changes its policy or if there's a slowdown in the global market. Perhaps the impact of any of these changes on product risk might have already been investigated; perhaps only a halfway job has been done. Cutting through with pertinent questions can help produce some answers.

This proves once again how useful diversity in the governing body can be. I'm not talking here just about gender diversity; diversity of know-how and experience is also important. In my experience, if everyone on the governing body thinks they all have the same know-how and the same kind of education, no-one will dare to ask searching questions. The director asking the question soon gets the impression that s/he's putting fellow directors who have the same know-how under pressure. This is where a supposedly 'naive' director can play a role: when s/he puts this kind of question, it is not seen as threatening and may therefore find its mark.

HELPING TO ENSURE MORE OBJECTIVE DECISION-MAKING

A critical-minded director can help to make decision-making more objective. It's vital that a governing body looks at a problem from a number of different angles. What impact will the decision have on the company's financing and risk position? Is the existing management able to execute the decision? What consequences will there be for the environment? What level of staff training will be required to implement the decision? Will the decision lead to a staff surplus? What short- and longer-term reactions will be triggered among the competition? How will the public authorities and the regulator react?

These are just a few of the questions that the governing body can put to management. Formulating questions both more broadly and more specifically leads to more in-depth decision-making. This is something that a company needs and this is something that the board of directors can deliver. More in-depth analysis, greater knowledge of the strategic options and consequences naturally make for better decisions, even when the governing body is not making the decision itself, but is merely there to approve – or even just discuss – a proposal. Discussions in the governing body can lead the CEO and the management to adjust the decision. In this way, more objective decision-making can be achieved. It's not only the opinion of the CEO or the management that counts.

BRINGING IN KNOW-HOW FROM OTHER COMPANIES AND MARKETS

I argued above that it's not very smart for a director to refer too often to other companies where s/he serves as director, CEO or manager, and give the impression that everything is better there. This can lead to resentment and earn the director a reputation as a 'know-all'. But it can be very helpful when directors can share knowledge from outside – without violating professional secrecy, of course. A director can help a particular manager by providing him/her with references and benchmarks, so that s/he can better assess whether the company is out in front or lagging behind with the activity in question. In addition, country and market information can also be useful to the company. However, professional discretion must take priority. When knowledge and insights are transferred, information can quickly become outdated and lose its value. Anyone who had a given experience at another company ten years ago should assume that much has changed since then and that this information is probably now worthless.

> Directors can bring knowledge into the company from outside, as long as it's not out-of-date.

Directors' emoluments

What kind of remuneration can directors expect to receive? Shouldn't good directors share in the profits – or receive part of the value – of a limited company? Sometimes shareholders find this an appealing principle, especially when the profits and value of the company are falling. Shareholders may believe that this makes directors more directly accountable – that they ought to 'feel the pain' which the shareholders themselves experience as a result of falling profits, losses, or value erosion. I don't agree with this view, as I will explain in the following paragraphs.

In principle, directors should not decide on their own emoluments; that decision will be made by shareholders at the AGM. The meeting will discuss a proposal from the governing body regarding the total amount of directors' remuneration and will then either approve or reject it. At stock exchange-listed companies, the discussion will be about the total amount to be paid to the directors as a group. At non-listed companies and organisations, directors' remuneration will be decided unilaterally by the shareholders. Distribution to each individual director of the total amount of compensation fixed by the shareholders will follow a set of rules, and in principle should be the same for all the directors of the company or organisation.

Individual remuneration paid to directors is published in the annual reports of stock exchange-listed companies, so that everyone can see what a particular director earns for the board work performed that year. At listed companies, there is therefore little secrecy about directors' earnings. You don't find such transparency at companies not listed on the stock exchange, but experience shows that remuneration at a non-listed company is substantially lower. This makes sense, given the difference in the level of responsibility.

The composition and structure of directors' compensation are different at almost every company or organisation. Sometimes they receive a fixed annual payment plus a fee for attending each board meeting or committee meeting. These attendance fees are intended to encourage non-executive directors to take part in every meeting. However, non-executive directors will usually receive no variable compensation or bonuses linked to company profits or value. As I underlined above, I agree with this principle, although shareholders might well wish to see directors' emoluments linked to the value of the firm, in order to ensure that the interests of the shareholders and directors are closely aligned.

Non-executive directors of a limited company must take care to ensure that the accounts present a true and fair view of the company's performance, assets and liabilities. They also need to verify that the risks are in line with the stated risk profile. In addition, they're responsible for ensuring proper execution of the strategy. These duties are simply not compatible with a variable reward package linked to profits and asset value. The reasons are obvious. What motivation could there be to present an accurate picture of profits and assets if a director's remuneration is directly dependent on the profits and asset values as reported in the accounts? Even if the directors are completely honest, which I don't doubt, this might nonetheless give the appearance of a conflict of interest.

There are some well-known cases of listed technology companies where directors' remuneration, in the form of share options, was dependent on the company's stock market performance and where, after some time, it became clear that the company's revenue figures were not giving an accurate picture of the sales actually made. A governing body that may expect a bonus when company value increases may also be more inclined to go for risky investments in order to try to increase the value of the firm – certainly so when directors are rewarded via share options. Directors would then benefit from an increase in the value of the company but not 'feel the pain' if it loses value. They may not move to halt an unsuccessful strategy if they speculate that the market will turn and once again deliver profits for the company. These are all good reasons for not granting non-executive directors variable compensation packages linked to profits and asset values.

On the other hand, however, the executive directors, the CEO and the managers should receive variable compensation packages. This will motivate them to do everything necessary to obtain the best possible results for the company or organisation. The non-executive directors should then provide a counterweight to the executive directors as it will certainly not be in the interest of the non-executives on the board to manipulate figures, take major risks or support risky strategies against their own better judgement. The balance between executive and non-executive directors on the governing body should enable the company to go full steam ahead by granting bonuses to executive directors. This balance also means that the company will stay within agreed guidelines by paying fixed compensation to the non-executive directors.

To sum up

Becoming a good director doesn't happen of its own accord; it requires effort. A prospective director must ask him/herself five questions.

- Am I able to deliver added value to the company on whose board I'll be sitting? The added value may be in terms of the professional expertise that s/he brings to the table, specific insights into technologies, markets or countries that are relevant to the company, or general knowledge and experience that can help the governing body to fulfil its tasks at the company.
- As a director will I feel sufficiently involved in the company and will I take an active part in board meetings, putting questions and making comments?
- Will I be able to make a sufficient effort to prepare for the meetings and expand my knowledge of the problems and risks the company or organisation may be facing?
- Do I accept that the interests of the company must always take priority over those that I myself champion?
- Will I be able to comply with the code of confidentiality pertaining to directors?

If a person can answer 'yes' to these five questions, s/he will undoubtedly be or become a good director. But s/he can only succeed in his/her role as director if the company or organisation plays its part as well. In this regard, a director can expect three things:

The company must give directors correct and, above all, relevant information in a timely fashion. It's foolish to overwhelm them with packets of paper or gigantic computer files which they will have to delve into to find out what has been happening at the company. It's far better for the company to focus on relevant information, and to be completely open about any problems it's facing.

Companies and organisations need to trust their directors. Hiding problems from directors in order not to alarm them doesn't solve anything. When you put your trust in others, they will trust you. If the company fears that a certain director cannot keep information confidential, it would be better not to appoint him/her in the first place.

A company needs to understand that directors are part-time workers and that consequently they will need to be reminded now and again about what a given problem is all about. It may well be frustrating for the CEO and management to have to listen for the umpteenth time to a presentation or take part in a discussion that they have already held in the management committee. Nevertheless, good directors will always add something to a discussion. And when they finally have to reach a decision, it certainly helps if that decision has been well prepared.

CHAPTER 10

The role of the governing body in the future

Will there still be a role for directors to play?

How is the role of the board of directors going to change in the future? What sort of profile will directors need to have? To answer these questions properly, we'll have to look into how companies are likely to change and, above all, how company shareholder structures will change, because the role and duties of a governing body are of course closely linked to what happens to the company or organisation.

It may surprise the reader that I intend to speculate here about how governing bodies are likely to change. Many people will assume that the duties, structure and way of working of a board of directors are stable elements in corporate life. However, this is not the case. Just because the obligation for every limited liability company to set up a governing body is enshrined in law, that doesn't mean that those governing bodies aren't subject to change. The law provides only a general description of the duties of a governing body and how it should operate. As I've indicated in the previous chapters of this book, the practical fulfilment of the tasks and workings of a board of directors is much more complex and depends to a very large extent on the context in which the board is operating.

It's true that company boards already existed way back in history. As I pointed out in Chapter 1, the council known as The Seventeen, which presided over the Dutch East India Company in the 17th century, was quite possibly the first ever board of directors in business history. However, I would say that boards, as we now see them at practically every company and not-for-profit organisation in Europe, only arose on a very large scale in the 1960s and 70s. They did of course exist before that, but almost exclusively at large, stock exchange-listed firms or companies that relied on funding from third parties.

Prior to the 1960s, it had been mandatory, for most company legal structures, to set up a governing body. Moreover, in addition to its general responsibilities, this 'board of directors' had to comply, by law, with a number of formal requirements such as drawing up a set of annual accounts and arranging formal delegation of powers. However, at a lot of small and medium-sized enterprises, these official requirements were fulfilled in a very formalistic and legalistic manner. The company accountant assembled the documents, got the directors to sign them, and the job was done. The board thus more or less met its legal obligations, but hardly any thought was given to a possible role in setting the course for the future. This was not bad policy or careless thinking; it was just practical convenience and it was perfectly legal. Company management felt no great need for a governing body, for reasons that will become clear in just a moment. We should remember that at that time practically every small or medium-sized company was still in the hands of a family, whose members performed most of the management jobs. These people were simultaneously owners, entrepreneurs and managers. They were of the opinion, sometimes quite rightly, that the board of directors was nothing more than a legal construct, an item of company law, but without any added value whatsoever as regards the manner in which they were then accustomed to working.

Then, as more and more shareholders who didn't actually work at these companies gradually took stakes in those businesses and they had to take out loans from banks and financiers, company management and strategic planning became more complex and the need arose for more dynamic and efficient governing bodies. The larger corporations had of course discovered this need a century earlier but during the 1960-1970 period it was the turn of the small and medium-sized firms in Europe. Gradually, the governing body at an increasing number of companies and not-for-profit organisations developed from a mere legal requirement into a genuine working body. Small and medium-sized companies were obliged to follow in the footsteps of the larger corporations, and the term 'governance' became a part of everyday management vocabulary. Having taken a look back at the recent history of corporate governing bodies, it's now quite interesting to try to predict how things will go from here.

In Belgium, the corporate governance codes that have been drawn up have played a big part in making companies aware of the importance of having a board of directors that works properly and is capable of assuming a course-setting role. A number of initiatives and projects have been undertaken. First was an initiative by employers' federation VKW, since re-named Etion. More important however was an initiative by VBO/FEB, the Federation of Enterprises in Belgium, supported by GUBERNA, Belgium's Institute of Directors, to draw up Belgian corporate governance codes. Drawing on the Code of Best Practice of Corporate Governance formulated by the Cadbury Committee in the UK in 1992, the VBO/FEB drew up first the Lippens Code, then the 2009 Code and now the 2020 Code. Also important is the Buysse Code, a code specifically developed for unlisted companies, which has helped to raise awareness of the importance of having a real board of directors at family-owned and other unlisted firms. There have also been a number of initiatives in the not-for-profit sectors such as universities and hospitals. However, further efforts will need to be made in the future on behalf of other non-profit segments. As these paragraphs will have made clear, you can only think about what might happen with regard to company governing bodies if you know what's likely to happen to company structures. I should, therefore, first describe the basic structure of a company or organisation. I'll do so by answering some fundamental questions. Once I've described the basic structure, I'll be able to start discussing how things used to be, are now and perhaps shall be in future and outline the consequences the changes are likely to have for the workings of the governing body.

Basic questions about the structure of a limited company or non-profit organisation

Every company or organisation is faced with four basic questions:
1. What is the purpose of the company or organisation?
2. Who has ultimate control? How does that control operate in practice?
3. Who bears the risks that arise from the strategy and dealings of the company or organisation?
4. Who exercises supervision?

A short explanation of each question will help to clarify the terms.

PURPOSE

I discussed the purpose or 'object' of a company or organisation in Chapter 4. This has become a very important concept in modern thinking about what companies and institutions actually do. Larry Fink, the highly influential CEO of the investment company BlackRock, described purpose as follows: "*It is a company's fundamental reason for being – what it does every day to create value for its stakeholders.*" In principle, there shouldn't be any contradiction between purpose and profit. Just because a company is pursuing a particular purpose that doesn't mean it will give up trying to be profitable. However, the profit motive is not in itself the purpose of the company. Profitability is absolutely vital but not in itself sufficient.

Purpose is about stating what the company basically intends to do for society at large and for those who are involved with or affected by the company, i.e. its stakeholders. Profit says something about how the company is going about achieving its purpose. If the firm fails to make enough profit, makes no profit at all or books a loss, this means that certain parties who are involved in the company are not getting the rewards to which they're entitled. The shareholders are losing part of their financial injection into the business or are not getting a fair return on their investment. By 'fair' I mean the return that investors would expect to make from a similar type of enterprise with the same risk profile. This means that in the long run they won't be willing to go on with this company.

Insufficient profitability also tends to get passed on to the employees, who may well find themselves being paid less than what they could earn at other companies. It will then become even more difficult for the company to recruit or retain staff, unless they can be compensated in some way for the poorer remuneration, by making job content more attractive than elsewhere, for instance. Pursuing a purpose that doesn't allow the company to make a profit also means that the company won't be able to grow because it won't be able to finance expansion or attract capital. Purpose without profit is unsustainable, just as profit without purpose isn't sustainable because it will ultimately undermine the commitment of the employees and weaken the allegiance of stakeholders and society at large.

CONTROL

Control is all about who ultimately has the power to make decisions at a limited liability company or not-for-profit organisation. Who determines the corporate purpose, vision and strategy? Who decides the amount of resources the company will have at its disposal, and in what form – based on debt or equity capital? Who decides on the dividend to be distributed to shareholders? Who has the last word when it comes to appointing executive management? Control is not about the little day-to-day operational decisions but about the big decisions that will shape the future of the company.

You won't always find control in exactly the same place at a company or organisation. It's useful to make a distinction between formal – or theoretical – control and de facto or actual control. In theory, the AGM always has the last word on all big decisions at the company or

> In theory the AGM always has the last word but very often the pater familias is really in control of the company.

organisation. However, the balance of power or distribution of power at the AGM can be such that actual control is in the hands of certain individual shareholders or lies with other bodies at the organisation. For instance, at a family firm, de facto control may lie with the 'pater familias' or key family members who hold a majority of the shares. At other types of companies or non-profit organisations, it's clear that the governing body or the executive management is really in control, which is often the case at listed corporations where the shareholder structure is highly fragmented.

Traditionally it's the distribution of the equity among the shareholders that determines who has control. A shareholder or block of shareholders that holds, or is able to control, a majority of shares in the company will exercise control over the firm. A shareholder or block of shareholders that has permanent control over the firm is known as the controlling shareholder or sometimes the 'reference shareholder'. The advantage of a system where control over the company is vested in those who hold a majority of the shares is that any shareholder who has, or wishes to acquire, control over the firm will have to make the biggest investment in the enterprise. Whoever has invested the most in the enterprise, and consequently also carries more risk than others, has the deciding vote. The disadvantage of this system is that it doesn't establish stable control over the company. It remains a fact that the largest shareholder has the option of selling his controlling stake to other parties and thus changing the control exerted over the company. In many countries, corporate law imposes criteria to the effect that transferring control in a way that is detrimental to other, non-controlling, shareholders will not be permitted, or in order to protect the interest of employees or the national interest.

In recent years, there has been intense discussion about company control and the possibility of establishing a system whereby a stable majority of shareholders could exercise control over a given company.

It's obvious that many entrepreneurs, company founders and some shareholders would prefer to structure the company in such a way that they can retain control over the firm without holding a majority stake. This has given rise to a debate about the desirability of issuing different classes of shares and shares with multiple voting rights attached. Issuing different classes of shares means that some shares come with greater voting rights while others are granted lesser rights or no voting rights at all, in this case compensated by attaching special dividend rights. Different classes of shares can also be reserved for particular people or institutions.

Entrepreneurs and company founders – especially at technology companies – endeavour to ensure they can retain control over the enterprises they created when they go out looking for extra capital to finance the growth of the business. However, we increasingly hear the desire expressed at other kinds of company as well to find a way to stabilise control over the company by creating different classes of shares or multiple voting rights. The argument frequently put forward is that this approach promotes sustainability and long-term thinking. This is certainly a positive thing for the company and the wider society. Nevertheless, there are two disadvantages. First and foremost, this approach undermines the principle of shareholder democracy – i.e. one share, one vote – and secondly it will, as a consequence, be harder to call the current company control into question if the reference shareholder abuses his position or allows the business performance of the company to slip. I don't think there's any ideal solution here; every situation must be looked at separately. It will therefore be essential to maintain the trust of those shareholders who don't have control or don't have any say within the group that holds control over the business.

Nowadays, social and environmental pressure groups also clamour to have some degree of say in what companies and not-for-profit organisations do. I've already discussed this point in a previous chapter. In my opinion, it's desirable and indeed necessary to take into account the views of these groups but I don't think it's advisable to create a formal system for receiving input from parties who don't have any stake in the risks and results of the enterprise.

RISKS

Any company will be faced with a variety of risks. The business plan may misfire because market conditions turn out to be different from what managers believed. Customers may refuse to settle invoices or simply be unable to pay. Suppliers may deliver late or not meet the required quality. The operational efficiency of the company or organisation may also leave something to be desired. Most parties that are involved with the company or organisation have signed a contract, they know what they're supposed to deliver and how much they'll be paid for that. Consequently, they don't bear any of these kinds of risks. Risks are basically borne by shareholders or whoever provides the company with risk capital. Banks or financiers that provide loans and investors who purchase the firm's bonds don't run any short-term risks because they have a signed agreement specifying the repayment at maturity date and the return they will obtain for making those funds available. On the other hand, risk capital providers don't have a fixed agreement; all they have is their expectations of success and the hope that the venture will turn out well.

Basically, the risk capital providers guarantee the commitments made with all the other involved parties. They guarantee payment of employees' wages, settlement of supplier contracts, payments to lenders and bondholders, and all the other risks. If the company is unable to meet all these commitments, then in principle it will go bankrupt and lenders and bondholders, employees and suppliers will all have a major role to play in deciding the following steps the company takes. The shareholders will have lost both their capital and their influence over company policy and activities. The lenders and bondholders will be first in line to be compensated, although workers' rights will need to be taken into account as well.

So it would appear that the risks are borne solely by the shareholders. This is certainly true in the short term. However, in the longer term, a number of other parties will be running risks, because lenders and bondholders will not be paid and employees will lose their jobs if the company or organisation is not able to achieve its purpose in a profitable manner.

SUPERVISION

Who exercises supervision over the use made of the resources provided by the company's shareholders and bondholders, over the hiring of employees, and compliance with the legislation and regulations in force? These are in fact just a few of the areas that require monitoring and supervision. As explained in the foregoing chapters, nowadays the governing body is responsible for this. However, there are other parties involved as well. External auditors, internal auditors and risk managers all play an important part these days as, inter alia, advisors to the governing body and the shareholders.

THE EVOLUTION OF THE LIMITED LIABILITY COMPANY

In the course of company evolution, four functions – determining corporate purpose, control, supervision and bearing corporate risks – have become increasingly split off from one another and turned into independent functions within the organisational structure. Originally all these responsibilities lay with the shareholders. They determined the corporate purpose, controlled the company – provided that they held a majority of the shares – bore the risks and organised supervision. Gradually, however, the need arose to split these functions up.

As more and more shareholders came on board, and when these shareholders were not closely involved with the company, as is the case with shareholders in listed companies, the need arose for independent supervision, not least because at that same moment effective control over those companies began to shift from shareholders to the management, a phenomenon to which Berle and Means[15] had already drawn attention in 1932. The main responsibilities of shareholders in listed companies consisted of exercising supervision over the management through the AGM and the board of directors – and taking action in the event of any major shortcomings – and bearing the risks.

This model held up for a long time, but then major changes came at the end of the 20th century and the early years of the current century. Companies appeared – mainly family-run firms, and mainly in Europa and Asia – which were floated on the stock exchange, but where a block of shareholders – known as the 'reference shareholder' – wanted to keep full control of the company. So basically, they needed a governing body that was essentially in the hands of the reference shareholder but able to act in a credible manner so as to win the trust of the non-controlling shareholders. Subsequently, companies appeared which had several blocks of shareholders. This phenomenon arose mainly due to the advent of private equity players, whose approach was to take large stakes in unlisted companies owned by several blocks of shareholders. The duty of the governing body was to set the course for, and exercise supervision over, the enterprise. The various shareholders sat on the board of directors and brought in independent directors so as to ensure that the board had credibility and also to bring additional expertise into the firm.

When large tech companies appeared and were launched on the stock exchange, a further split in the basic functions occurred. Entrepreneurs who set up this kind of company needed to turn part of their assets into liquid cash and still attract fresh funds to match the risks run by the enterprise. They therefore had to turn to the

15 Berle, A. & G. Means – *The Modern Corporation and Private Property.* Transaction Publishers (1932). Reprinted.

stock market but wished nonetheless to retain absolute control over the businesses that they had founded and nurtured.

The solution that they came up with consisted of issuing different classes of shares. In practice this means that not all shares issued by a company are equal. A Class A share will enjoy greater rights than a Class B or C share. This is predominantly a US phenomenon (though this practice has also been current for some time outside the USA, mainly in risk capital centres), but we can't rule out the possibility that it will become popular elsewhere. This policy of issuing shares of different classes enabled the founding entrepreneurs to retain control over their company and its purpose without having to hold a majority of all issued shares. At the same time, they were able to ensure that the corporate risks were borne by shareholders who had no control over the running of the company. One may suppose that those shareholders were prepared to accept these conditions because they had a lot of trust in the business sense of the founding entrepreneurs and were confident that the value of the shares they held would increase. In fact, they took on a large part of the risks without having much say in how things were run, but they did have the prospect of considerable gains.

Recent economic history has shown that their trust and confidence was justified in this respect. More recently, society has shown rather less trust in tech entrepreneur-founders because their technological innovations have been making serious inroads into personal privacy and the way society is organised, but a correction to this tendency will surely be found. The governing bodies certainly have a very special role to play at these companies. They have the job of steering the companies in conjunction with the founding entrepreneurs and exercising supervision so as to ensure protection for those shareholders who have fewer rights. It's therefore vital that these directors should have an untarnished reputation. If anything goes wrong on this front, this form of company will find it hard to survive.

Three types of companies

Going forward, I think that – continuing an evolution which has already begun – the corporate world will see the development of three major types of company (see box). The category into which companies fall will be largely determined by their size and structure, their need for different types of financing and their consequent relationships with the holders of their stock. As we have seen throughout this book, these typologies, and the shareholder structures and contexts pertaining to them, will call for different types of governing bodies, and require directors with various different profiles.

The company of the future: three types

- Type 1: Large stock exchange-listed companies, mostly in the hands of a few super-sized investment funds, hedge funds or pension funds. They will operate worldwide and their shareholders will be professional investment funds and those investors who still invest directly in company securities. There will usually no longer be any dominant or reference shareholders invested in Type 1 corporations.
- Type 2: Closed companies that will tend to be no longer listed on the stock markets but go forward with one or more reference shareholders, who might be family groupings or specialist investment companies. In addition, a number of investment companies might have minority holdings in the firm.
- Type 3: Fast-growing technology companies that are listed on a specialised stock market. Going forward, they may perhaps grow to become Type 1 corporations. Alternatively, such companies might accept a takeover bid or, after some time, morph into a Type 2 company.

Type 1 companies will be very large corporations, usually operating on a global scale. They will need to be listed on a stock exchange because the capital they'll require in order to finance their assets and operations cannot be provided, and the risks that will have to be taken cannot be borne, by investment companies, private equity funds, individual shareholders or family wealth structures. Another reason why Type 1 companies will need to float on the stock market is that a liquid market is always important for investors and the stock exchange is a proven instrument for liquidating investments when necessary.

Major listed corporations will increasingly find their shares in the hands of investors who will not really act like 'genuine' shareholders. These investors will only be looking at financial indicators relating to the securities issued by companies – i.e. risk-return ratio, volatility, (beta) correlation with market indices and market liquidity, to name but a few.

The duration of an investment in a stock exchange-listed company can be just a few seconds, in order to profit from a sharp movement in the share price, or several days, weeks or months. It's highly unlikely that in the future, stock market investors will act as stable shareholders in large companies. They'll tend to buy shares in major listed corporations and sell them again according to movements on the financial markets and events at the firm. Increasingly, non-professional investors will turn away from buying company-issued securities directly and will invest via funds set up and run by professional asset managers so as to benefit from their expertise in portfolio analysis, securities analysis and diversification. Except where these investment professionals opt for a 'buy and hold' strategy, the key point will be to try to buy and sell at just the right moments. The way in which these professional investors will exercise control over the company will quite simply be by buying and selling their shares on the stock market or futures market.

> The duration of an investment in a listed company might be weeks or months, but sometimes just a few seconds.

There are strong indications that major (Type 1) corporations will increasingly be regarded as investment products which professional investors use to invest savings they've collected from a variety of wealthy and not-so-wealthy people. As I mentioned above, these professional investors can hardly be regarded as genuine 'shareholders' in the companies concerned. This development already started a few years ago, is already in full swing and is now speeding up. The process is perhaps a little slower in Europe because over here there are quite a lot of small 'retail' investors who still prefer to invest directly in the shares of various types of company, but even they are also gradually switching to invest their savings, great or small, in professional investment funds.

In addition to these listed corporations, whose shares will increasingly be bought and sold by professional investors, we'll find a large number of Type 2 companies. These are typically medium-sized – although it's difficult to say what 'medium-sized' means in precise figures – companies with a completely different shareholder structure. They tend to have a nucleus of patient long-term shareholders – typically one or more core shareholders or 'reference shareholders' exercising control and often intervening in the decision-making process – alongside a number of other shareholders. Today the core shareholders are often families or investment companies that draw on family wealth or rely on capital raised from professional investors or smaller stock market investors. At the present time, the non-core shareholders in this type of firm are often investment companies which specialise in buying and holding for a number of years significant minority stakes, some professional investment funds, plus a number of minority shareholders, who nowadays in many cases invest directly through the stock market but in the future will for the most part go through investment companies or funds.

I believe that in the long term these smaller companies will simply disappear from the stock markets, either de-listing from the stock exchange or rejecting the idea of an IPO in the first place. There are three main reasons for this:

Stock market investors will become less interested in buying the shares of small companies because, in comparison with the really large corporations, fewer and fewer stock market analysts will continue to track their stock. The cost of having research done by specialist analysts working for financial institutions is high. Recouping this cost is becoming increasingly difficult, given that liquidity for these shares on the stock market is low, with infrequent and low-volume trading. Those who invest in this type of company risk getting trapped in a firm where a shareholder with only a small stake has no real control.

Investors will no longer need small or medium-sized companies to achieve diversification in their portfolios, as stock will be available in a sufficient number of large companies to enable efficient investment portfolio diversification.

The kind of blocks of shareholders who are invested in such firms and wish to have their voices heard in the running of the business will not wish to sit on the board alongside representatives of stock market investors. They will also regard the mass of regulations associated with a listing on the stock exchange – though imposing comprehensive regulations on listed firms in order to protect investors who buy shares on the public markets is of course not unreasonable – as a restriction on their freedom of action. Regulation on listed companies has become so extensive that the advantages of a listing for medium-sized and small companies are diminishing or disappearing altogether.

Following this trend, small and medium-sized companies will increasingly have a controlling shareholder alongside a number of investment funds, which will of course have far-reaching consequences for the governing body.

The third category of company (Type 3) will consist of technology startups – fast-growing enterprises that are generally financed from the very beginning through funding from venture capitalists. Often achieving expansion via specialist exchanges such as, for instance, Nasdaq, these growth-oriented companies will probably remain key to the growth and development of stock markets. Launching the company on the stock market through an initial public offering (IPO) gives venture capitalists a chance to reap the rewards of their (risky) investment.

Meanwhile, an IPO also provides a tech company with an opportunity to explore what its future might be. Underpinned by the stock market, the enterprise may be able to grow independently into a major listed corporation like the Googles, Amazons, Facebooks and Microsofts of this world. Alternatively, the founders and owners might accept a takeover bid from another firm which needs their technology and market position in order to keep growing, and the two companies may thus move forward together. If this is the founders' intention, then the stock market can serve as a sort of shop window where the company can be objectively appraised and valued. Of course, it's also possible that after some time the tech company's core or reference shareholder(s) might decide that growth can better be achieved as a private company; it may therefore move over to join the Type 2 category.

These three kinds of companies will have different types of governing body. I'll go into these in just a moment. But first I'd like to talk about a phenomenon affecting companies that will be, or already is, of fundamental importance for the role of the governing body.

The new social engagement

The three sorts of companies I've described operate in a capitalist system that is increasingly being called into question. I don't think that the majority in society would wish to call into question the market mechanisms that are fundamentally linked to capitalism, but there is certainly a call from society at large for a transition to a form of capitalism that is more responsible and inclusive. In practice, this means that people expect a company to behave in a way that promotes a fairer, more sustainable, world. A company can make this happen by being caring and inclusive towards its employees, taking into account the impact of its activities on the environment and the climate, delivering products and services that truly add value for its customers, achieving profits for those who've invested in the company, treating suppliers fairly, improving the area where it's located or does business and not imposing costs on locals which cannot be recouped, and last but not least by paying a fair amount of tax. Companies of all types are increasingly likely to be faced with questions about their social engagement and responsibility. This will have an effect on the role that the governing body will play going forward.

Changes in the governing body

If, as I expect, companies will basically break down into the three types I described above, their governing bodies will also undergo changes. Below is an overview of each type.

GOVERNING BODY OF A TYPE I COMPANY

Type I companies will typically be listed on the stock exchange and their shareholders will be mainly professional investors. These investors won't really be involved in the company but will exercise their power by buying and selling shares on the stock market or the futures market. The duty of the board of directors will thus consist mainly in promoting investors' trust in the securities issued by the company. The board will first and foremost be a supervisory body and its role in setting the course of the enterprise will be sharply diminished. This course-setting role will fall to the executives of the company; i.e. the CEO and the management team. Indirectly the board will provide guidance when the CEO has to be replaced or a failing strategy needs adjustment. However, its key task will be to promote investor trust.

This will have consequences for directors of Type I companies. First and foremost, they'll need to have an excellent reputation. This may stem from their business know-how, their successful career at other companies, their integrity, or their ethical conduct. Institutional and professional investors want to be able to count on company directors, so the directors will continually have to ensure that the company complies with all applicable laws and that they have the agency problem under control, so that the management use company resources economically and don't enrich themselves through misuse of funds. In addition, the directors will need to ensure that the company behaves in a responsible manner in society.

Today regulators in Europe are already carefully monitoring the appointment of directors at banks and require that bank directors be 'fit and proper'. By 'fit' they basically mean that directors must have a thorough knowledge of the business of banking; 'proper' means that they must have a good reputation in terms of ethical conduct and compliance with laws and regulations. In some European countries, directors also have to sit exams. In the future, it cannot be ruled out that bank directors may need to obtain certification before they can become eligible for a seat on the governing body of a large bank.

For the moment, there are no such rules and controls for other kinds of companies. However, if a major violation of investor trust were to occur, imposition of such rules could not of course be ruled out. Meanwhile, the regulators ought to ensure that companies are taking steps to ensure sufficient diversity on their governing bodies.

> If directors are all clones of each other, the governing body will lack depth.

Gender diversity can easily be monitored. However, the board of directors of major listed companies should also demonstrate diversity of knowledge, experience and culture. Directors of a bank should not all be former bankers. Similarly, the directors of a chemicals company should not all be chemists. When directors are all clones of each other, the governing body will lack depth. At the other extreme, however, if directors know nothing about the business that they're supposed to be monitoring, this obviously will not promote in-depth debate in the decision-making process either. So it's vital to strike a good balance between specialist knowledge of the company's technology, customers and markets on the one hand and diversity of know-how and experience on the other.

GOVERNING BODY OF A TYPE 2 COMPANY

The governing body of a Type 2 company will, in comparison with that of a Type 1 company, have a more pronounced role in setting the course of the enterprise. Directors will discuss, together with the CEO and management, the strategic direction which the company should be taking. This Type 2 board will also exercise the supervisory and monitoring role. But because it's quite likely that the directors in a Type 2 scenario will have close contact with the company, they will be able to observe at first hand what's happening with the company's assets.

The directors on the governing body of a Type 2 company will often either be shareholders or else direct representatives of blocks of shareholders. However, there will also be a need for independent directors on the board. There are three reasons for this. Independent directors will be needed in order to keep the balance between the various shareholder blocks and thus to ensure that conflict between shareholders doesn't escalate. They will also have to take care that minority shareholders are treated fairly and that minority interests are not sidelined. Lastly, independent directors usually bring additional know-how and experience from other sectors and businesses that are useful for the company. It will frequently be the independent directors of a Type 2 company who do most to build up the company's network. Independent directors can moreover help to encourage more socially responsible behaviour.

GOVERNING BODY OF A TYPE 3 COMPANY

The governing body of a Type 3 company will also play a more course-setting role than the board of a Type 1 corporation. This is because a technology company will generally be financed by venture capitalists who have put their money into the enterprise with few or no guarantees and therefore want to be able to exercise close supervision over the business. They'll want to control the company in conjunction with the founding entrepreneurs.

The board of directors of a Type 3 company will therefore be mainly composed of the founding entrepreneurs and venture capitalists, plus a number of independent directors who are able to endow the tech company with credibility. In cases where the firm's shares are being traded on a specialised stock market, these independent directors will be important for engendering trust among the investors.

The presence of representatives of venture capital on the board means that the company will be strongly motivated to increase its value, as the venture capitalists will be looking to achieve a return on their investment from an increase in company value. Dividends will not generally be distributed, as all available resources will be needed to develop the technology and build market share. This also means that investors who have bought shares in the business on the specialist stock exchange will also be driven to achieve a capital gain because they won't be receiving any dividends and will have to obtain a return on their investment through rising company value.

All concerned, the founding entrepreneurs as well as the other groups of investors, will be well aware that a Type 3 company is basically a business in transition that might be taken over by another firm or grow into a technology giant and eventually become a Type 1 corporation. It will be the role of the independent directors on the board to maintain a balance between the venture capitalists and the founders, plus also to bring in additional know-how and help to create market openings. It goes without saying that having independent directors on the board is important for the company's reputation and image on the stock markets.

The future of governance at not-for-profit organisations

So far, I have focused exclusively on the way the governing bodies of for-profit companies might change in the future. However, I think the role of the governing bodies of not-for-profit organisations such as hospitals, cultural institutions, sports associations, universities, social welfare organisations and even NGOs is also likely to change.

Although those kinds of non-profits have so far been run with a great deal of idealism and goodwill, there have – fortunately – been some changes since the beginning of the century in the way they're supervised. After several cases of financial wrongdoing – basically the result of shortcomings on the governance side – came to light, there began a number of initiatives to draw up codes designed to ensure better governance in the not-for-profit sectors. I confidently expect that over the next few years much more attention will be devoted to improving and professionalising – in a sensible manner – the governance of non-profits. There are three reasons for this.

The first reason is that the providers of funds to these organisations are no longer prepared to accept a situation where no proper control is exercised over the use of funds and resources conferred by the public authorities or obtained from sponsors and donors. Members of the governing body of a non-profit will need to be aware that they are accountable for the use made of the available resources. The time when funds were pumped in blindly in all good faith is over. Donors and sponsors like to stay involved with organisations to which they've given money. They like to hear and see how the organisation is endeavouring to attain its targets with the resources they've provided.

Non-profits that receive money from the public purse are of course generally monitored by government-appointed commissioners or delegates but we're entitled to wonder whether this is an effective way of maintaining supervision. Government commissioners are not always professional supervisors and they're sometimes not even genuinely independent. My biggest objection to their role is however that they tend to elbow the board of directors aside. Government commissioners, especially in Belgium, take into their own hands the control that's supposed to be exercised by the board of directors, with the result that the directors don't really feel responsible any more for the use of resources. Nor do the public authorities talk to them on the subject. Many public authorities seem to regard the governing body as a superfluous body that's only useful for handing out jobs. I certainly hope that the authorities are now gradually beginning to realise that change is needed and that governing bodies at not-for-profit organisations ought to be taking on their full responsibility, as is the case in the business world.

A second reason why I expect that those governing bodies are heading for some changes – in Belgium and perhaps also in other countries as well – is that nowadays not-for-profit organisations are entrusted with more complex tasks. Cultural institutions, hospitals and universities, to mention only these three, have become complex organisations that are expected to carry out sophisticated activities and they need to make considerable investments in order to stay up-to-date. A lot of non-profits are larger, in terms of jobs, budgets and capital investment, than many privately-owned companies or even listed firms so it's only logical that these institutions should also have a professional governing body.

The third reason to expect change at the governing bodies of not-for-profit organisations is that they'll be expected to be more transparent about the workings of the organisation. Listed companies are accustomed to making public announcements about their results, balance sheets and compensation packages. This is still not usual at non-profits – although there are some honourable exceptions to this general statement.

Corporate governance codes in the future

Corporate governance codes have helped to drastically improve and professionalise the role and workings of the governing bodies at both for-profit companies and not-for-profit organisations in a number of European countries. Moreover, the introduction of the 'comply or explain' principle has provided the opportunity to create flexible practices, enabling companies and organisations to apply the basic principles while adapting them to reflect each organisation's individual circumstances. As I pointed out in Chapter 2, there can be huge differences between one board of directors and another because the context within which boards have to operate can vary sharply from company to company and organisation to organisation.

The most important contributions made by codes such as the 2009 and 2020 Belgian Corporate Governance Code and the Buysse Code is that they've encouraged the governing bodies in Belgium to make structural adjustments. The list of recommended changes to the structure of governing bodies is rather a long one, including: separating the roles of board chair and CEO; not appointing the current CEO to succeed a departing chairperson; appointing independent directors to the board; setting up committees reporting to the board of directors; drawing up charters setting out how the board of directors and each of the committees should operate; and recommendations on the composition of committees. The structural changes recommended by the governance codes set in motion a process of change for governing bodies. The codes have improved the way the board of directors works but have also resulted in less attention being paid to the conduct of directors on the board. This became clear in the wake of the 2008 financial crisis. When investigations were carried out into how corporate governance was being exercised at the banks at the time of the crisis, it rapidly became clear that the banks had good governance structures in place according to the currently applicable corporate governance codes. Where things had gone wrong was the way directors had behaved within those structures. They appear to have been insufficiently informed and much too pliable.

The problem wasn't the structures; it was the way people behaved within those structures. The regulators have tried to do something about this but it's much easier to draw up rules about structure than rules of behaviour. Measures relating to banks have been taken, such as the introduction of the 'fit and proper' rules, which are designed to indirectly bring about changes in directors' behaviour. However, it's obviously impossible to impose an obligation on directors to have the courage to ask critical questions and to keep on asking if they don't receive an adequate answer.

> During the 2008 banking crisis the problem wasn't the structures; it was the way directors behaved within those structures.

Will corporate governance codes still exist in ten or fifteen years' time? I'd like to answer 'yes' to this question but I'm not at all sure. Discussions have been going on between legal experts for years now about 'soft' law, such as codes, and 'hard' law such as company law. The proponents of hard law see a great advantage in enforceability and the fact that legislation has a clear field of application. The opponents of hard law argue that codes offer flexibility and the opportunity to adapt rules to the context in which any individual governing body has to operate. On the other hand, it's clear that judges will take the precepts set out in the codes into account in their rulings whenever investors are counting on the fact that these codes will be applied. This seems to have been the case in the 'Fortis case' brought in Belgium in 2008-2009, when investors won their case because the judges ruled that the Fortis corporate governance statement should be treated as more or less equal to the company statutes.

From discussions with politicians I've learned that they're generally somewhat cooler towards corporate governance codes, largely due to the 'comply or explain' principle. Politicians tend to see this principle as too non-committal. They say that it sounds as though if you fail to comply with a certain point, you simply have to explain why...

and that's that! This is of course not the case. A lot of codes, including the 2009 Belgian Corporate Governance Code, have an appendix intended to clarify what is meant by a 'good explanation'. The new (2020) version of the Belgian Corporate Governance Code takes a clearer, more precise, position vis-à-vis the new Company Law – first and foremost including in the Code precepts on directors' behaviour which didn't find their way into the legislation. So there's a clear distinction between hard law and soft law and more thought can be given to the principles to which a director ought to adhere as regards his/her behaviour in the governing body. The 2020 Belgian Corporate Governance Code has made the difference between legislation and codes even clearer.

I think that these codes will remain useful because they enable flexible compliance with corporate governance principles. As far as Type 1 companies are concerned, I think the various stock exchanges ought to get together and try to draw up a single common code. The Americans are certainly not likely to jump at this idea but it should be possible to do so within Europe. The advantage would be that professional, and other, investors will then know what they can expect from major listed corporations in terms of corporate governance.

Three challenges

I think that, going forward, governing bodies will face three challenges. First and foremost, there is the stealthy 'judicialisation' of the governing body. Second comes the difficulty they will face in finding good directors. And lastly, there are the fundamental changes that are making huge requirements on the governing bodies of companies and organisations.

JUDICIALISATION

As a consequence of incorporating a large number of directors' obligations into legislation and corporate governance codes, there is a now a strong tendency among companies to entrust the formulation and monitoring of corporate governance to corporate lawyers or specialist advisors. This can be useful as a stop-gap measure, to ensure that directors are thoroughly informed about what is expected of them. Nevertheless, as I underlined earlier in this book, a governing body is not at all like the jury of an ice-skating competition, whose members each give a separate, individual assessment, expressed as a number, of the performance of each skater, based on the rules of the discipline, without any consultation with the other judges.

The initiative and the responsibility for exercising corporate governance must lie with the governing body itself and – first and foremost – with the chair. The chairperson and his/her fellow directors need to work out how, with the help of a code that's suited to their situation, they can arrange the best possible corporate governance for the company or organisation. The board chair and the other directors need to take joint responsibility for good governance and shouldn't let themselves be led by the hand by lawyers, who usually have a very academic and legalistic knowledge of governance but often lack practical know-how.

Another danger arising from the 'judicialisation' of governing body work is that directors may find themselves working from a sort of 'to-do list', essentially performing a 'box ticking' exercise. Under this approach, the board tries to find a solution for applying the various principles set out in the codes and the requirements laid down by law. Governance then becomes like getting a card stamped: have we fulfilled all the conditions? This is of course an important question, but directing a company or organisation is certainly more than this. As I underlined in Chapter 1, it basically consists of setting the course for the company or organisation, supervising and monitoring, setting standards and taking responsibility for everything the company does.

Lists can help you to perform these tasks, just as pilots use checklists to prepare for take-off. But flying is more than just ticking off points on a list.

FINDING THE RIGHT DIRECTORS

A lot of managers and investors feel the call to become a company director. Nevertheless, to (mis)use a famous quote: "many are called but few are chosen". The problem is that board directors need to embody a combination – consisting of specific knowledge and experience plus a relevant network – that is uniquely suited to the activities of the company but at the same time quite general. Directors must be able to deliberate with their fellow board members about strategy, technology, operations, human resources policy, environmental requirements, potential acquisitions, company finance and the management. They must be able to formulate and argue an opinion about some of these matters and at the same time be able to judge whether what their board colleagues and the management say on the other subjects sounds reasonable. Moreover, board members should not be executive types who sit in the boardroom feeling frustrated because they would much rather go out and take matters into their own hands. Company directors need specific expertise but must also be able to think in more general terms and provide advice without intervening themselves. Not everyone has these abilities; the job requires a special character.

A CHANGING WORLD

One last challenge is that nowadays company directors are faced with a rapidly changing society. This is partly due to digitalisation, which is disrupting business models, products, technologies, customers and distribution channels, but there is much more than this going on, as I've indicated in this and other chapters of the book. The society in which companies and not-for-profit organisations operate is very different today. The role of the company is being called into question – often unjustly, because the contribution which companies make to society by developing new technology, serving customers' needs and creating jobs is not always recognised or correctly valued. However, board members are certainly expected to ensure that decisions they take or green-light will help to improve the lot of all stakeholders.

To sum up

The role of governing bodies and the directors who sit on them – whether at a for-profit company or a not-for-profit organisation – is set to change. The reasons are obvious: the context in which those organisations operate is going to change radically. Directors will become more professional. That doesn't mean that they'll become more specialised but they'll become more skilled, more expert, from a general management point of view. A group of narrow specialists isn't going to be able to improve the performance of a governing body.

Companies will change and their relationship with their shareholders will change as well. Some large corporations will become like investment products into which ordinary investors can put their money through specialist investment funds. Other firms will be capitalised by blocks of shareholders who are closely involved with the company. Both these developments will have consequences for the way the governing body works.

There is now political pressure to turn the job of director into a certified profession. I don't believe this is a good thing as regards promoting diversity on the governing body. The most important thing is without a doubt that any board of directors must be suited to the company it's supposed to serve. Governing bodies of not-for-profit organisations are set to change as well. Greater transparency in the governance process will be necessary. Governing bodies are now becoming more professional, but they need to go further along this path.

I leave the reader with one last thought: governing bodies will have to make sure that the for-profit companies or not-for-profit organisations they serve assume their social responsibilities. This is the only way to ensure that those organisations retain their credibility in the society of today and tomorrow.

This book was originally published as
Geheimen van de bestuurskamer, LannooCampus, 2019.

D/2020/45/163 – ISBN 978 94 014 6382 9 – NUR 800, 805

COVER DESIGN Sarah Schrauwen
PAGE DESIGN LetterLust | Stefaan Verboven
TRANSLATION Chris Boothby, SeaBee Communications
PORTRAIT PHOTO Frederic Sablon

LannooCampus Publishers is a subsidiary of
Lannoo Publishers, the book and multimedia division
of Lannoo Publishers nv.

LannooCampus Publishers
Vaartkom 41 box 01.02   P.O. Box 23202
3000 Leuven   1100 DS Amsterdam
Belgium   Netherlands
www.lannoocampus.com